EXPLORING

THE LIFE, MYTH, AND ART OF

THE

SLAVIC WORLD

CIVILIZATIONS OF THE WORLD
EXPLORING
THE LIFE, MYTH, AND ART OF
THE
SLAVIC
WORLD

CHARLES PHILLIPS AND MICHAEL KERRIGAN

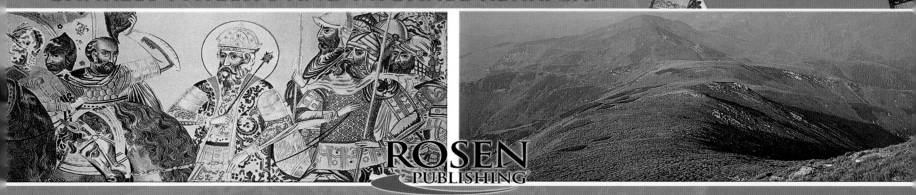

ROSEN
PUBLISHING
New York

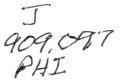
5 0503 01109478 8

This edition published in 2017 by:
The Rosen Publishing Group, Inc.
29 East 21st Street
New York, NY 10010

Library of Congress Cataloging-in-Publication Data

Names: Phillips, Charles.
Title: Exploring the life, myth, and art of the Slavic world / Charles Phillips and Michael Kerrigan.
Description: New York : Rosen Publishing, 2017. | Series: Civilizations of the world | Includes index.
Identifiers: ISBN 9781499463965 (library bound)
Subjects: LCSH: Mythology, Slavic--Juvenile literature. | Slavic countries--Social life and customs. | Slavic countries--History
Classification: LCC BL930.P48 2017 | DDC 299'.18--dc23

Manufactured in China

First published as *Forests of the Vampire: Slavic Myth* by Duncan Baird Publishers, text copyright © 1999 Duncan Baird Publishers.

Contents

THE SLAVIC WORLD

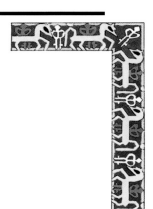

In the early sixth century AD, Slavic tribes burst from obscurity into the bright light of recorded history. Their progress was irresistible as they poured southwest over the Carpathian Mountains on the borders of modern Ukraine and Romania into the Balkans. Chroniclers from the Byzantine or Eastern Roman Empire called these warriors "Sclavini". They moved on foot rather than horseback and avoided fighting in the open, specializing in ambush and stealthy night attack. Expert river navigators, they were also strong swimmers and were renowned for their ability to hide underwater for long periods by breathing through reeds held in their mouths. Procopius, the sixth-century Byzantine historian, recorded that the Sclavini herded prisoners of war together with their cattle and sheep and ruthlessly put them all to the torch. But this "Slavic migration" was by no means always warlike, for in many places the incoming Slaves mingled quite peacefully with settled tribes.

Opposite: **Despite the later pre-eminence of Novgorod and Moscow, Kiev's role in Slavic history is reflected by buildings such as the 11th-century cathedral of Sancta Sophia.**

From the fifth to the seventh centuries there was a great movement of peoples which increased Slavic influence across the continent, but as the Slav tribes spread east, west and south from their homeland, they gradually became isolated from one another. Scholars have identified three main groups: East Slavs, in Ukraine and Russia; West Slavs, in Poland, the Czech Republic and Slovakia; and South Slavs, in the Balkan peninsula.

These people spoke a common language as late as the ninth century, but it was transformed through interaction with other tongues and has become the mother of thirteen modern languages including Bulgarian, Croatian, Czech, Polish, Serbian, Ukrainian and Russian. But for all the diversity produced by a long and often bloody history in different geographical regions, the Slavs share an ancient inheritance that has been passed down across the centuries from the days when they scratched a living on the soils of the great eastern European plain. This rich cultural heritage is celebrated in the countless oral epics, songs and folktales that remain a powerful force in the Slavic imagination. Whether revering mythic heroes or articulating a firm belief in the reality of mischievous spirits, the stories and beliefs that the tribes took with them, and developed over generations, offer insights, both magical and terrifying, into the make-up of the Slavic soul.

Above: **The Carpathian Mountains formed a formidable western boundary to the lands of the early Slavs. Beyond them, however, to the south and west, lay plains that many Slavic tribes would, centuries later, claim as their own.**

Dark Plains of Destiny

The struggle for a homeland amid the vast central European plain was, for countless ancient tribes, a long and fruitless one. But of the peoples who battled for survival in the forests and steppes between the Elbe and Volga rivers, few proved as enduring as the Slavs who settled the entire area through a process of tribal conquest and cultural assimilation. as the architects of the first great eastern European civilisation.

It is thought that the Slavs emerged from the southerly parts of the Russian plain, which stretches from the Baltic Sea in the north to the Black Sea in the south. Although Slavic tribes later spread out to the east, west and south, this vast expanse, marked by rivers and great forests, visited by cruel winters, scorching summers and rolling thunderstorms, must have remained etched into the sensibility of its first settlers, for it casts a brooding shadow across Slavic folklore and mythology. The forest regions have informed countless tales of lost children and travellers preyed upon by sylvan ghouls; just as the great wastes of open steppe offered a bleak canvas to the fertile imaginations of those who lived there.

The first humans, *Homo sapiens* – who developed in sub-Saharan Africa around 100,000 years ago and migrated north – explored parts of the Russian plain during a mild part of the Ice Age

Central Europe had already been populated for thousands of years and most tribes who crossed the plains had moved on, but the Slavs stayed. These images were painted in bat dung on the walls of Rabisa Cave in Bulgaria, c.900–400BC.

about 33,000–30,000 years ago. They were hunters of wild horses, reindeer, mammoths and other herd animals, and left the remains of many camps between the Dnieper and Don rivers.

For thousands of years such tribes of hunter-gatherers survived in northern and eastern Europe, migrating across the plains in search of better living conditions as the climate changed. Around 8000BC the first farming communities appeared in the Taurus Mountains of Turkey, the Zagros ranges of Iraq, and in Jordan. Over the following 2,000 years, people throughout the Near and Middle East learned the benefits of this new way of life, and farming reached the fringe of the European plains.

Radiocarbon-dating of sites suggests the first agricultural communities in the Balkans appeared in around 6000BC, and over the next three millennia farming settlements spread into parts of southern Russia and what we now know as Ukraine and Moldova. By the end of this period Europe was essentially divided between farmers in the south and west and hunter-gatherers in the north and east. Very roughly, the line of division ran north to south through what is now eastern Poland and then west to east through the Balkans and the forest-steppe landscape of Ukraine.

It was in the lands at the very limit of the farming world, in the forest-steppe areas of the plain, that the first Slavs emerged – and some scholars have tried to trace a cultural continuity from the first farming tribes in the third millennium BC to the early Slavs. But no one knows for sure the extent of this proposed continuity.

Over the following millennia many tribal groups moved across the Russian plain. The southerly steppes in particular formed a kind of passage linking central Europe and Asia, along which many nomadic groups travelled. These people would either settle the land and mingle with existing tribes or they would come intent on conquest. Inevitably, however, cultural ideas and trade accompanied tribal movement.

Greek colonies spread along the northern shores of the Black Sea in the seventh to fifth centuries BC, and the farmers of the forest-steppes traded with the new arrivals, exchanging grain and

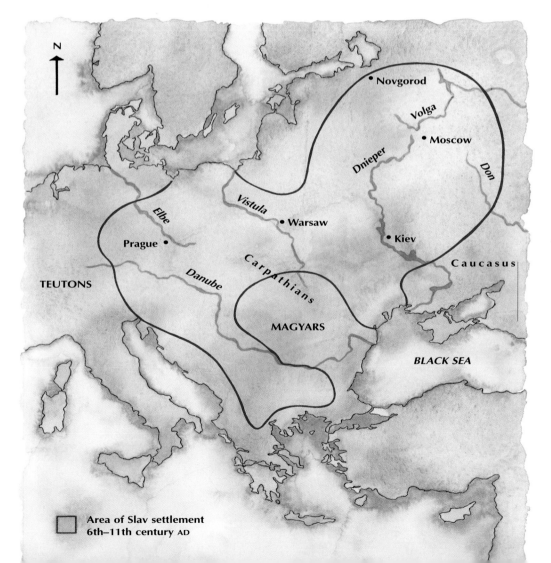

The Lands of the Slavs

The boundaries of the Slavic expansion are marked by rivers and mountain ranges. From the Ural Mountains in the east to the Elbe River in the west, Slavic tribes overcame servility to successions of invaders to become the dominant group in central Europe. Their influence even spread as far south as Greece. The rise of the Magyars, southwest of the Carpathians, however, served to separate the Slavs into isolated groups, which meant that those in the east, west and south would develop quite distinct cultural and religious identities.

Area of Slav settlement 6th–11th century AD

From Oral Tradition to Written Texts

Russian oral epics – or byliny **– are part of a tradition that runs back into the shadowy prehistory of the Slavs. These songs survived for centuries without being written down.**

Many of the epics still existing today were composed in the tenth to twelfth centuries, the glorious era of Kievan Rus. They tell of the heroic warriors who built up and defended the first Russian state against aggressive nomads like the Polovtsians and Pechenegs, who swept westward along the southern steppes. These Russian heroes or *bogatyri* – a word possibly derived from the Turkic *bahadur*, or warrior – include Ilya Muromets, who was born a cripple but cured by pilgrims, thus enabling him to become a mighty warrior. Dobrynia Nikitich, mainly remembered for killing the dragon, was another fearless vanquisher of the pagan hordes.

The *byliny* remained an oral tradition after the coming of literacy with the Christian Church. Writing and reading were not the province of peasants but of priests and monks, who were enemies of anything pagan. The first written records of *byliny* and historical songs, therefore, were not made until the mid-eighteenth century when Kirsha Danilov was hired by a mill owner to research the folklore of the remote Ural Mountains. A century later a Russian civil servant, Pavel Rybnikov, published more than 200 *byliny*. He had discovered them in Petrozavodsk (in far northwestern Russia, near the Finnish border).

In the mid-nineteenth century, Russian folktales also became popular. Writers such as Alexander Afanas'ev and A. F. Gil'ferding published successful collections of stories. The tradition of singing *byliny* flourished until World War II but the telling of tales lives on today.

The epic battles of the Kievan kings remained a favourite subject for Russian artists into this century. Here Igor fights the Tartars, from *The Tales of Igor and his Sword*.

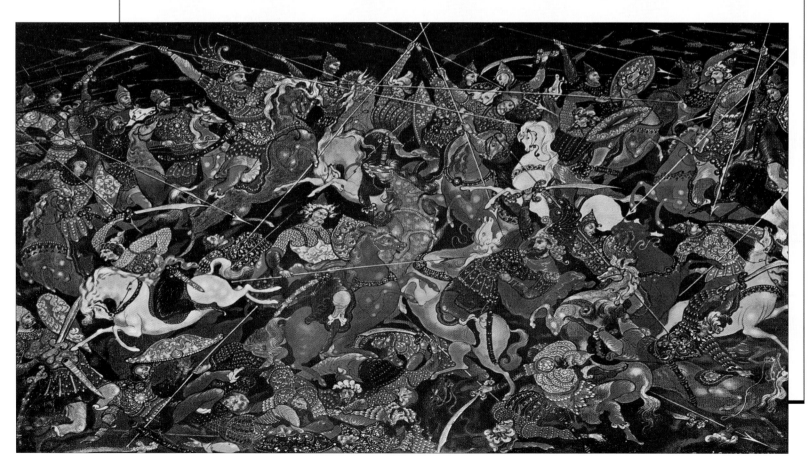

vegetables for Greek wares such as amphorae and bronze goods. The establishment of the Roman Empire in the last two centuries BC brought stability and good roads which further boosted trade. Although the empire never took control of the forbidding plains, its eastern borders were not closed and in times of peace traders and travellers from "barbarian" tribes beyond the frontier journeyed to its thriving markets, acquiring perhaps a little Greek – the language spoken in the Eastern Roman Empire – as well as cultural influences. Some scholars argue that the farmers of the forest-steppe region in the last centuries BC spoke an early version of the common Slavic language and might even be direct ancestors of the Slavs.

By the fourth century AD, the Roman Empire was in decline. A shortage of labourers, caused by various epidemics and ever-rising recruitment into the army, led to a falling away of agricultural production and a weakening of the empire's powerbase. On the fringes of the empire, tribes were becoming increasingly restless, sensing easy pickings in the Roman provinces which remained much wealthier than the lands beyond the frontier. Germanic tribes, led by the Goths, soon swept across the open plains.

In the fourth century AD, the lands of the Eastern Goths were overrun by the Huns — mounted pastoralist tribesmen from the parched desert-like lands of central Asia. In the wake of a heavy military defeat in 376AD, the Goths and their subjects capitulated. The Huns began to build up a large empire, which at its height, under Attila, stretched from the Danube far across the steppes to the Caspian Sea and Caucasus Mountains. When Attila died in 453, however, the empire collapsed and into the temporary power vacuum marched ambitious tribes from the west and east, intent on claiming these coveted lands as their own.

Trade and animal husbandry offered tribes such as the Slavs alternatives to a life ruled by warfare. This Scythian gold pectoral, *c.*2nd century BC, depicts people milking sheep and fashioning shirts from hides. But the terrors of the plains are also shown, in the form of beasts tearing at one another's throats.

The Origins of the Slavs

Among the subjects of the Goths and Huns were groups of people who have been identified by many scholars as Slavs. These fifth-century tribes no longer lived as nomads but as farmers in settled communities, growing crops of wheat and millet while raising cattle, pigs, sheep and goats. They followed the comparatively advanced agricultural techniques practised in Roman provinces – using manure and crop rotation as well as the wheeled plough. They worked with sickles, scythes, axes, ploughshares and knives made of iron.

Their settlements were mostly unfortified and built alongside rivers, although they left some remains of fortified camps, with timber palisades and ramparts, on higher ground. Their houses

11

TIMELINE	30,000–1 BC	AD 1–450	AD 450–850

Amid the ever-changing cultural landscape of eastern Europe, the Slavs do not emerge as a clearly identifiable group until about the 5th century AD. Their subsequent history, however, is more clearly recorded; and the establishment of the first great Slavic state, Kievan Rus, is now the stuff of legend.

Below: *Eastern European gold animal figure, c.7th century BC.*

c.30,000 BC *Homo sapiens* begins to roam the Russian plains.
c.8000 BC Farming communities settle in the Taurus Mountains.
c.6000 BC Nomadic herdsmen arrive in the Balkans.
c.5000 BC Agricultural settlements spread into southern Russia.
c.700 BC Greek colonies establish themselves along the shores of the Black Sea and begin trading with people of the steppes to the north.
c.200 BC Growth of the Roman Empire sees roads built and trade boosted along its eastern borders.

Above: *Bronze plaque from the Crimea, c.4th century AD.*

330 Emperor Constantine moves his capital from Rome to Byzantium.
c.400 Huns precipitate the decline of the Roman Empire. Slavs living in settled communities under Goth/Hun rule.
453 Attila the Hun dies and his empire collapses.

c.500 Slavic tribes migrate south, west and north. Slovenes settle in the northern Balkans.
550 Sclavini threaten Thessalonika and Constantinople.
578 Tiberius becomes emperor of Byzantium and aims to bring Slavic tribes under control.
c.580 Slavs and Avars overrun the Balkans.
c.625 Emperor Heraclius signs a treaty with Serbs and Croats of the Carpathian Mountains to protect his capital.
626 Constantinople withstands siege mounted by the Avars, Sclavini and Persians.
c.670 Bulgar raiders sweep into Balkan peninsula.
681 Bulgars sign treaty with Constantine to protect Byzantium.
c.700 Emergence of the first towns across the Russian plain.
800 Czechs rule Bohemia. Charlemagne awarded the title of Holy Roman Emperor.

were square in shape with part of the building set underground. Ovens were made of stone and walls built of earth and timber. Archaeologists have shown that these simple huts would not have lasted long and were presumably often moved and rebuilt. Settlements, each containing up to twenty-five houses, were built close to each other in groups of three or four. Remains of Slavic villages of this era have been found between the modern Czech and Slovak republics and the Dnieper River.

The Slavs lived in extended family groups headed by a father or grandfather. This "house father" acted as a pagan priest for the family and was revered after his death – for ancestor worship was an important part of Slavic paganism. Women, who took charge of cooking and child-rearing, were led by a "house mother" who was usually the wife of the house father; their children worked in the fields from a young age. These people lived in a cluster of small buildings which would surround the home of the house father. They united in clans which together formed tribes, ruled by a *zupan*, or chief, and a council of prominent men.

There are contemporary historical accounts of the early Slavic tribes. Among them were the Sclavini and the Antes, mentioned by the sixth-century Roman historian Jordanes. He said that the Sclavini occupied land between the Carpathians, the Vistula River (in modern Poland) and Dniester River (in modern Ukraine), while the Antes lived further east between the Dniester and Dnieper rivers. The lands of the Sclavini, he said, stretched far away to the north and were made almost impassable by thick forests, forbidding rivers and marauding beasts. They lived in makeshift huts and when attacked would abandon their villages and hide in the impenetrable forests and swamps.

AD850–1020

869 Death of Cyril.
870 Bulgaria converts to Christianity.
882 Oleg seizes Kiev.
884 Death of Methodius.
896 Hungarians overrun lands north of the River Danube and establish Moravia.
950 Emergence of unified Polish state under Mieszko I.
955 Kiev's Princess Olga converts to Christianity.
988 Vladimir accepts Christianity as state religion.
1015 Death of Vladimir. Murder of his Christian sons, Boris and Gleb.

Left: *Saints Boris and Gleb became the first Russian martyrs when they were murdered by their pagan half-brother Svyatopolk in 1015. School of Moscow, c.1340.*

AD1020 on

1049 Cathedral of Sancta Sophia finished in Kiev.
*c.***1054** Kievan Rus, the largest federation in Europe, established.
1112 Nestor compiles the *Russian Primary Chronicle*.
*c.***1130** Kievan state begins to split into smaller principalities.
1169 Andrew Bogolyubsky sacks Kiev. Power shifts northwards to Moscow and Novgorod.
1240 Mongols take Kiev.
1382 Russian independence focused on Moscow after its sack by Mongols.
1544 Ivan IV "The Terrible" becomes first Tsar of Russia.
1682 Peter I becomes Tsar. Emergence of secular literature.
1861 Tsar Alexander II abolishes serfdom in Russia.

Below: *An icon of Ivan "The Terrible". From Grand Duke of Muscovy, Ivan IV assumed the title Tsar after unifying the Russian state and expanding it to the shores of the Caspian sea.*

In the sixth century, Procopius described the Sclavini and Antes as tall, with ruddy colouring and spirits hardened by their austere lifestyle. Many references suggest that they were productive farmers. The Byzantine writer Pseudo-Mauricius said that the Sclavini harvested wheat, millet and other grain and kept many cattle. According to other sources, they used canoe-like boats carved from tree trunks and were fond of mead and a strong drink made from honey and barley.

There are even earlier written references to tribes which some have identified as Slavs, despite the lack of hard evidence. In the first century AD a group named the Venedi was mentioned by the Roman historian Tacitus in his *Germania*. He described them as wandering robbers active between the eastern Carpathian Mountains and what is now eastern Russia, and said that they carried shields and fought on foot rather than on horseback. In the first century AD, the Roman scholar Pliny the Elder mentioned the Antes as inhabiting an area near the Sea of Azov (just north of the eastern end of the Black Sea) and the Caspian Sea. Later, Jordanes suggested the Venedi, Antes and Sclavini were all of the same blood.

The second-century AD Greek writer Claudius Ptolemaeus, or Ptolemy, wrote of the "Soubenoi" – a form of "Slovene" or "Sclaveni" when transliterated into Greek – in his *Geography*. He said they lived alongside Asiatic tribesmen west of the Ural Mountains. Ptolemy mentioned another tribe sometimes identified as Slavs, the Serboi. According to his account, they had settled on the northern fringe of the Caucasus peaks (which run along Russia's southern border with Georgia). The accounts are incomplete and contradictory, but nevertheless provide tantalizing pointers as to the movements of the peoples later identified as Slavs.

13

The Slavic Migration

In the fifth and sixth centuries AD, Slavic tribes began moving out from the Russian plain to the north-west, east and south, leading to the wide dispersion of Slavic-speaking groups throughout eastern Europe and the Balkans. The reasons for the migration were varied: over-population would have necessitated a search for new lands, while rising temperatures and decreasing rainfall were also inflicting punishing droughts on the forest-steppes and making productive farming of the area increasingly difficult. The Slavic-speaking farmers must have learned some of the arts of warfare from the successive waves of invaders who had imposed harsh rule on them – and this would have made aggressive expansion a viable option.

Most tribes travelled to find land to settle and tribes to conquer. But the Slavs were essentially different from other raiders classified by Byzantine and Roman historians as barbarians. The Huns and Goths were nomads whereas the Slavs were farmers and stock-breeders with an essentially settled way of life, tied to the land. Various historians emphasize that when the Slavs expanded as a military force it was in tandem with other, dominant peoples – for instance, the invasion of the Balkans was carried out with the Avars, and the Slavs were essentially their subjects. This suggests that the large-scale Slavic movements were of farmers coming in the wake of the raiders, settling and planting lands that had been drenched in the blood of their earlier occupants.

According to a number of scholars, the Slavic expansion in certain directions was essentially a spreading out of influence and culture. New lands were assimilated as more tribes learned to communicate in a common Slavic language. The success of the Slavs' sophisticated agriculture and the economic power that derived from it fuelled their movement. Nomadic, warlike peoples, on the other hand, were unlikely to have had such a deep and enduring influence, which may explain why the Avars, while leading the assault on the Balkans, had no lasting impact on the area.

A silver cup with a horse-shaped handle, made around the 1st century AD by the Sarmatians, a warlike people who aimed to profit through conquest rather than trade. Under their leadership, Slavs were later to venture into the Balkans.

Serbs, Croats and the Balkans

Some writers suggest that the first Slavic migrations to the southwest were undertaken as pressed auxiliaries in the forces of the Sarmatians – one of the groups of Asiatic nomads that settled the Russian steppes, and in the fourth century overran the Hungarian plain. There is evidence that Slavs were among the raiding forces of the Huns a century later. Jordanes recorded that on the death of Attila a funeral feast called a *strava* was held. Scholars have established that this was a Slavic word.

At the end of the fifth century AD, the focus of much military campaigning in eastern Europe was Byzantium (also known as Constantinople, today's Istanbul). Slavic tribes – the Sclavini and probably the Antes – are known to have taken part in barbarian raids into the wealthy Byzantine Empire throughout the fifth and sixth centuries.

In the second half of the sixth century, the Avars took control of land that stretched from modern Hungary and Romania, through the middle Danube, right up to the Elbe River.

Emperor Tiberius (578–582), wanting to bring an end to raids by the Sclavini into Byzantine territories, persuaded the Avars to wage war on them. The fighting did not last, however, and the two tribes soon became allies. In the 580s and 590s, they overran the Balkans, reaching southern Greece and even the Aegean islands. From this time on, contemporary writers referred to the Balkans as "Sclavinia" – the territory of the Slavs.

In the late 620s, Emperor Heraclius made an alliance with the Serbs and Croats, two tribes living north of the Carpathian Mountains. They are both generally identified as Slavs, but some scholars consider the Croats to be of largely Iranian stock. Byzantine forces helped the Serbs and Croats invade the area inland from the Dalmatian coast (on the Adriatic Sea) to expel Avars and Bulgars who had been harassing Byzantium. Serbs and Croats then settled in the area, mingling with Slavs and non-Slavs who were already living there. Another Slavic tribe named the Slovenes settled in the region of the Sava River in the northern Balkans, the area of modern Slovenia.

Slavic tribes also moved into the eastern lands of the Balkan peninsula (modern Romania and Bulgaria) in the sixth and seventh centuries. In the 670s Bulgar raiders swept into the area, having been driven southwest from the steppe lands north of the Black Sea by the Khazars, a group of Turkic-Iranian peoples settled in the Caucasus. The Bulgars overran the Slavs, but also mingled with them, and the two groups rapidly developed a joint culture. In 681 they signed a treaty with Emperor Constantine IV, under which their independence within the empire was recognized. In the early ninth century, Bulgar-Slavs expanded into land north of the Danube and south into Macedonia (northern Greece). From this period on, Byzantine writers made no distinction between the Slavs and Bulgars in the region who had, by then, merged into a single Slavic people, the Bulgarians.

Byzantium's influence on the East Slavs was profound. Here the Emperor Theophilus, who was crowned in 821, makes a proclamation, flanked by his bodyguards who include Russians, in a scene from the 10th-century *Scylitzes Chronicle*.

The West Slavs were influenced by Teutonic rather than Byzantine culture, affecting their language, religion and art. This bronze-gilt buckle is from Greater Moravia, in what is now the Czech Republic, *c.*9th–10th century.

A Western Frontier

Slavic peoples travelling westwards came into contact with local Germanic tribes and, through a process of assimilation and conquest, were settled north of the middle stretches of the River Danube (in the modern Czech and Slovak republics) from the sixth century. Despite the constant incursions of the Avars they were able to consolidate Greater Moravia after Charlemagne's destruction of the Avar lands in 796, and its princes Mojmir and Rotislav converted these lands to Christianity.

To the northwest (in what is now the western Czech Republic), the Czech tribe ruled the state of Bohemia by around 800. This area lay on an important trade route between the Baltic and North seas and the Adriatic. This route was much favoured by Germanic merchants who provided an influential link with territories to the west. By the eleventh century the Western rather than Eastern form of Christianity had established itself there.

This spiritual rift was then compounded by geographic isolation. When nomadic Hungarians, the Magyars, overran the lands north and south of the Danube (modern Hungary) in the decade after 896, they occupied Slovakia (an area equivalent to the modern Slovak Republic), and developed a culture quite different from that of the Slavs. The Hungarians' language, Magyar, was not assimilated by the local tribes. Like Finnish and Estonian, it was a "Uralic" language descended from a mother tongue spoken in the area around the Ural Mountains (now central Russia) some seven millennia ago. The Hungarians and their language thus developed in isolation from their neighbours and separated the West and South Slavs, whose dialects, in turn, began to develop independently.

Other Slavic tribes spread northwards from the Carpathian Mountains (in northeast Romania and southwest Ukraine) to settle the fertile plains watered by the Oder and Vistula rivers. In the late ninth century, much of the territory came under the rule of Greater Moravia and, in the mid-tenth century, the first unified Polish state emerged under the Christian leader, Mieszko I.

Traders of the Eastern Fringe

From the sixth century, Slavic tribes moved northwards seeking new land where they could farm and breed stock. As they went they discovered plentiful supplies of honey, wax, timber, furs, amber and, in the villages of smaller tribes, slaves. They gradually developed a network of trade and influence exploited by armed bands of traders who criss-crossed the Russian plain.

The spread of settled farms and the growth of trade led to the appearance of the first towns on the Russian plain during the eighth century. Tribal loyalties were strong among nomadic groups, but they fell away as people's livelihoods became centred on the rapidly emerging settlements.

Trade routes began to link the Baltic and the Black seas: in Scandinavia the prosperous Vikings provided an eager market for luxury goods and for honey and furs. The staging posts for these lucrative trade routes were groups of farmsteads that formed the basis of the first towns. As trade had to be protected from bandits, most of these places were fortified by the ninth century. Merchant-warriors formed a new elite focused on protecting their own interests. Towns soon developed into major centres for the surrounding countryside, offering professional craftsmen a secure place to settle and make a living.

Kiev benefited from the lucrative trade routes that opened up between the Baltic and Black seas. Merchants and craftsmen moved into the area, trading items such as this bronze and enamel brooch, from Crimea, c.6th–7th century.

One of these prosperous settlements, Kiev on the Dnieper River in modern Ukraine, became the centre of the first Russian state – Kievan Rus. Although its period of pre-eminence was brief, from the ninth to the twelfth centuries, it has assumed towering importance in Russian collective memory as a golden era, partly because during this time the coming of Byzantine Christianity brought with it a great flowering of culture. Its reputation echoes down the ages, through the Mongol occupation of parts of Russia and into the imperial and revolutionary eras.

Viking merchant-adventurers, known in Russia as Varangians, played a key role in the birth of the Kievan state. They appeared in northwestern Russia in the first half of the ninth century, intent on winning control over the lucrative trade routes that ran across the region. But scholars are unable to agree as to whether the Varangians founded Kievan Rus, or merely developed it.

According to the oldest of the Russian chronicles, Nestor's *Povest' Vremennykh Let* (the *Tale of Bygone Years*, or the *Primary Chronicle*), written in the eleventh century, the tribes of the Russian plain drove back the first Varangian incursions but then fought bitterly among themselves and asked the Varangians back to rule over them. Three brothers of a Scandinavian tribe called "Rus" came to establish order. The eldest, Rurik, eventually took control and built the town of Novgorod on Lake Ilmen. Oleg (882–912) succeeded Rurik and, moving south with troops in 882, seized Kiev. The fledgling state was a loose confederation of principalities, with rulers controlling their own areas but owing allegiance to the Grand Prince in Kiev.

One of the principal aims of Nestor's *Primary Chronicle* was to glorify the achievements of the dynasty descended from Rurik and Oleg, and so its account of the origins of Kievan Rus must therefore be treated with some caution.

Archaeological remains reveal that Kiev was already a leading Slavic settlement when Oleg took control. This fuels the argument between Scandinavian and Russian scholars, in which the former give the Varangians total credit for creating Kievan Rus while their Russian counterparts deny that the Varangians played a significant role. Some of the most recent scholarly opinion argues that the state existed in an embryonic form when the Varangians arrived, but that the incomers gave a vital impetus to its development. Whatever the roots of the state, its growth is clearer.

Oleg launched the first attempts to win more territory for Kiev. They were continued by his successor Igor (912–945) and with remarkable initial success by Igor's son, Svyatoslav (945–972). Svyatoslav defeated first the Khazars in 968 and then the Bulgars, who settled to the east around the Volga. He also came to the aid of the emperor in Constantinople in his conflict with the Bulgars of the Danube region. Svyatoslav willingly drove them out and even established the Kievan capital in their principal city, Pereyaslavets, for two years. But in 971 Svyatoslav failed in a bid to invade Byzantium. As he returned home, he confronted an army of Pechenegs, Asiatic nomads who were threatening the Kievan state from the east. Svyatoslav was defeated and killed on the banks of the Dnieper River. The nomads' leader, Kurya, took no mercy on his opponent, issuing the dread command that Svyatoslav be beheaded, his skull scraped out and lined with silver – and then put to use as a drinking cup.

Vladimir (from 980) and his son Yaroslav (from 1019) went on to seize land in the northwest (now part of Poland), and in the tenth century Russians began moving east from the Novgorod-Kiev river route, driving out or assimilating Finnish tribes that lived in the area of modern Rostov, Vladimir and Moscow. At Yaroslav's death in 1054 Kievan Rus was the largest federation in Europe, stretching north to south from the Baltic to the Black Sea and east to west from the Carpathians to the region of modern Moscow. Under Grand Prince Oleg, the Russians reached Byzantium in 911 and agreed a trade treaty which led to the Kievan fleet helping Byzantine military campaigns as far afield as Syria and Crete. In return the Kievan state received the trappings of trade and culture which would endure for centuries.

Life in Kievan Rus

Trade brought wealth to comparatively few in Kievan Rus. Most of the people were not merchants but farmers who survived by growing crops and raising stock animals. They also kept bees for honey and some went out fishing and hunting. From the *Pravda Ruskaia* (*Rus Justice*), a legal code from the reign of Yaroslav, it is clear that the first Russians kept cows, sheep and pigs and grew wheat, hemp, rye, millet, garlic, cabbages and turnips. In some areas farmers still practised partly nomadic slash-and-burn agriculture but this tended to be on the more isolated fringes of the state. Elsewhere they used field rotation and manuring. Historians refer to a number of "towns" in Kievan Rus but, apart from Kiev, Novgorod, Pskov and Tchernigov, these were no more than village markets set in a vast expanse of swamps and forests.

Most of the farmers were free men, known as *smerdy* ("stinking ones"). They were able to pass their land on to their sons, although the *Pravda Ruskaia* declared that all land ultimately belonged to the Grand Prince. His officers collected tribute from the farmers, often in the form of furs, honey or grain, which they then sold for themselves.

The princes maintained groups of officials – *boyare* – as a military force and as administrators. Some of them were Scandinavian and others were probably leaders of the local Slav tribes. Originally the *boyare* had no connection to the land but increasingly they became landlords. They would rent equipment and small areas of their land to peasant farmers who were also required to work on their lord's fields. As farmers began to fall into debt, the movement towards the enslavement of the peasants as serfs began – and it gained momentum with the spread of large estates.

The practice of collecting tribute, however, was a provocative gesture much resented by those whose existence was far removed from city life. It

The last of the Rurik kings, Fyodor I, is celebrated in a 16th-century icon. The dynasty survived the fall of Kiev and lasted until Fyodor's death in 1598.

often provoked conflict. In 945 Grand Prince Igor was slaughtered by a band from the Slavic Drevlian tribe, who refused to accept a demanded increase in the tribute. His widow Olga – a decade later a gentle convert to Christianity – is said to have exacted terrible revenge. She killed two bands of Drevlians, burying the first alive and burning the second. Then she sent troops to the main Drevlian town of Irorosten, with orders to raze the settlement and slaughter its inhabitants. However, she may not have been quite so ruthless in reality: the details of her terrible revenge are taken from the account of a Christian monk who probably exaggerated the wickedness of her pagan years in order to emphasize the glory of her later

conversion to Christianity.

In a land with so many forests, wood was the main building material in Kievan Rus. Houses and even the majority of churches were built of logs. The people wore clothes of wool and linen, covered with fur in winter, and long boots. They were peasant farmers, living close to the earth on which they relied for daily sustenance. Many aspects of life for the Slavic peasant farmers who lived in Kievan Rus remained essentially unchanged right through to the the 1917 revolution. And this may explain why the spirits of the woods and fields proved equally enduring.

The Kievan state fell apart in the 1130s. Conflict between princes contributed much to the decline, but the most important factor was the dwindling of Kiev's importance as a trade centre. Trade routes were shifting, with more goods travelling by land through central Europe. In the south, new bands of Asiatic nomads swept through the steppe corridor, disrupting access to Byzantium and the empire. They also took part in Kiev's internal princely squabbles, further undermining unity. The centre of power gradually moved to the forested north, to Novgorod and Moscow. Then, in 1169, Prince Andrew Bogolyubsky of Suzdal sacked the city of Kiev. He returned triumphantly to his own lands in the upper Volga, and made Vladimir his capital.

A watercolour from *The Tale of Prince Michael* depicts Grand Prince Michael of Tver and his *boyare* distraught at the sight of Kiev in ruins. As decreasing trade and political infighting weakened the state, it was unable to recover its former glory.

The Coming of Christianity

In an age of great political uncertainty, when disparate tribes still roamed the European plains intent on short-term, bloody gain, strong central government and auspicious political alliances were becoming essential for the survival of any nascent state. Paganism, with its infinite regional variations, encouraged localized allegiances. Christianity, however, with its immutable doctrines written down as law, promoted spiritual, and thus social and political cohesion. The centres of the Christian world, Rome and Byzantium, were themselves eager to spread their influence into new territories and, since these places were the centres of most

Cyrillic Slav Languages

When Cyril and Methodius developed the first version of the Cyrillic alphabet in the ninth century, the Slavic peoples shared a common spoken language. Geographic isolation and differing cultural and religious influences, however, meant that diverse Slavic tongues were to develop over the centuries.

The Cyrillic alphabet that grew out of Cyril's and Methodius's missionary work gave the Slavs their first written language, although it was reserved for writing ecclesiastical texts. It was later called Old Church Slavonic, and had forty-three characters, most based on Greek letters or combinations of them. Some characters – such as the Cyrillic letters for "ts" and "ch" – derived from Hebrew.

The brothers probably grew up bilingual, for they were born and raised in the Macedonian city of Thessalonika, where both Greek and Slavic were spoken. They are also said to have learned Hebrew in 860 for a diplomatic and religious mission north of the Black Sea to the Khazars, who had converted to Judaism.

The Cyrillic alphabet used in modern Slavic languages has fewer letters – for instance Russian has thirty-two letters, Ukrainian thirty-three and Bulgarian thirty. Cyrillic is also used for a number of non-Slavic languages spoken in countries of the former Soviet Union.

When groups of Slavs became isolated from one another, however, their languages changed. Among the East Slavs, languages developed in three isolated groups: Russian, Belorussian and Ukrainian. The development of the West and South Slav languages was given impetus by the arrival of the Hungarians in the ninth century.

The Cyrillic alphabet was therefore unable to become a unifying force. It provided a single written language common

An example of Cyrillic script, from Serbia, c.14th century. While initially a pan-Slavic religious script, this form of writing came to indicate a purely East Slav identity.

to all groups within the Eastern Church, but it was known to and used by only a tiny ecclesiastical minority. In the wider context, it would even serve to divide the Slavs. Members of the Eastern and Western Christian churches used different alphabets, exacerbating religious divides.

European trade, many pagan leaders came to see the wisdom of closer links to Christendom. So in 862 Rotislav, Prince of Greater Moravia, asked the Byzantine Emperor Michael III to send Christian missionaries into his lands. The following year a party of monks led by two brothers, Constantine (later called Cyril) and Methodius, who were fluent in the Slavic language as spoken in their native Macedonia, arrived and began to preach the Gospel to the Slavs. They translated the Bible into Slavic and used the language in all their services. Constantine created a whole new alphabet known as Glagolitic to render Slavic in written form. After his death his Bulgarian disciples developed this into the Cyrillic alphabet that is still used for Russian and other languages today.

These advances led to the religious conversion of many Slavic countries: Bulgaria turned to Christianity in 870 and Poland established the country's first bishopric at Krakow in 969.

The Conversion of Prince Vladimir

In 988, under Prince Vladimir, Kievan Rus officially accepted Byzantine Christianity. Conversion had been a gradual process. The Christian faith arrived in the Kievan territories in the ninth and early tenth centuries but its first adherents were isolated groups among a pagan majority. Princess Olga, who became regent on the death of her husband Igor in 945, was baptized as a Christian ten years later. Her son Svyatoslav, however, rejected the new faith in favour of the old pagan ways.

The coming of Christianity had a profound effect on local arts and crafts as shown by this 12th-century book illumination from Prague depicting Bohemian saints, including Adalbert, Prokop, Wenceslas and Ludmilla, in heavenly Jerusalem.

Despite the deeds of Vladimir, Cyril and Methodius, shown here in a 19th-century icon from Veliko Turnovo, were credited with the forging of Slavic Christianity.

The monk Nestor in his *Primary Chronicle* tells how, before agreeing to convert to the Byzantine Church, Vladimir sent messengers to investigate the religions of the Muslim Bulgars in the region of the Volga River, the Byzantine Church and the Germanic tribes. According to his account, the messengers found no joy – and a bad smell – among the Bulgars and no beauty among the Germanic Christians. But they were overwhelmed by the elegance of the liturgy and worship in Byzantium, where they visited the magnificent Hagia Sophia, the "Church of Holy Wisdom", that had been built by Emperor Justinian in the sixth century and was already more than 400 years old.

A Greek metropolitan – an Orthodox archbishop – was stationed in Kiev as an emissary of the Byzantine emperor and of the Church patriarch. While this gave Byzantium no political power in Kiev it did indicate a significant cultural influence. Vladimir's conversion was a decisive moment in the history of the East Slavs, consolidating their movement away from northern and western Europe – and the Latin Church in Rome – and focusing their attention on the south and east. After the fall of Byzantium in the fifteenth century, the Russian state of Muscovy was to set itself up as the city's inheritor, safeguarding its spiritual heritage.

Byzantine missionaries and craftsmen poured into Kievan Rus, and played a vital role in shaping the emerging Russian culture. With Christianity came literacy. Translators and writers – mostly from monasteries – were active at the prince's courts, particularly in Yaroslav's reign, which saw a great flowering of culture. They translated the Bible and liturgy. They also composed annals and chronicles, which reflected a desire to see Russia as a unified land with a single history.

Such books might have been a valuable source of information on Slavic culture and religious life before the coming of Christianity had they not been written by Christian monks. As enemies of the old religion, they were not concerned with preserving tales of Slav heroes and gods. Slavic paganism never developed its own literature because literacy came only with Christianity. The old tales survived, if at all, through the folkloric tradition, handed down by word of mouth.

The Heirs of Byzantium

The most visible effect of Christianity was the appearance of religious buildings. In the immediate aftermath of Vladimir's conversion, Byzantine architects, working alongside Russian craftsmen, began erecting churches, cathedrals and monasteries throughout the Kievan state: the magnificent cathedral of Sancta Sophia was built in Novgorod in just seven years, commencing in 1045.

But it was in Kiev itself that most of the building took place. The Church of the Tithes was built from 989 to 996, while work began soon after on a highly ambitious cathedral, which was also to be dedicated to Sancta Sophia. It had five naves adorned with splendid mosaic portraits of the Russian princely elite. This celebration of Slavic Orthodoxy was built of marble specially imported from far-flung regions of Byzantium. Completed in 1049, it still stands today, a surviving jewel of Byzantine architecture and proof of the great cultural achievement that was Kievan Rus.

Chronicles describe this Byzantine-influenced city in awed terms. By the twelfth century, there were more than 400 churches in Kiev, and the city was also famed for its mosaics and frescoes and for the quality of its silverware.

Despite this, however, the stories which endure from this age focus on the warring heroes, Oleg, Ivan and Vladimir, reflecting the constant raids the city endured from Khazars and Pechenegs throughout its history. While Novgorod and Moscow became more famous for trade, both cities took their cultural cue from Kiev.

The conversion of pagan eastern and central Europe to the Christian faith widened the splits

The bell-tower of the cathedral of Sancta Sophia in Kiev remains the finest example of the architectural style that mixed Byzantine church design with Russian craftsmanship. Built in the 11th century, it marked the first flowering of Slavic culture.

between different groups of Slavs. Russians, Bulgarians and Serbs were tied to the Eastern Church; Poles, Slovenes and Croats to Roman Catholicism. Over the centuries to come, religious differences would even inflame conflict between Poles and Russians and Croats and Serbs.

But although cultural unity for all the Slavs was no longer a realistic possibility, there remained a surprising degree of continuity with the pagan past that led back to a shared culture. Ritual offerings of grain to the gods — made by the earliest Slavs, as we know from archaeological evidence — continued in some Slavic areas even into the twentieth century. Among the peasants the old beliefs of the pagan Slavs persisted, in time mingling with the new faith as pagan gods were identified with Christian saints. The ancient fertility cults of Mother Earth – in Russian, *Mat' Syra Zemlya*, "Moist Mother Earth" – fed into Christian worship of the Virgin Mary.

The Middle Ages and After

Remarkably, for many Slavs the pattern of day-to-day life set during the tenth and eleventh centuries changed very little until the nineteenth or even twentieth century. One reason for this was that serfdom in Russia was not officially abolished until 1861, by Tsar Alexander II, which meant that peasant lifestyles persisted for hundreds of years almost unchanged since the early Middle Ages. But the vast areas of open plain ensured that many rural communities were simply too far removed from the maelstrom of military and political change that affected city dwellers: the coming of Mongol invaders to Russia and of the Ottomans to southeastern Europe, religious wars in the Czech lands, the creation of great Polish and Russian empires, the rise of Communism and the erection of the "Iron Curtain" across Europe – all passed them by. The industrializing twentieth century may have wrenched many Slavs from the land, but as late as the post-revolutionary 1920s, farmers in northern Russia around Novgorod and Arkhangelsk were pursuing the slash-and-burn agricultural lifestyle practised by their remote ancestors. Over centuries, millions of Slavs – widely dispersed across central, eastern and southern Europe, divided by language and by religious differences – shared a hard life close to the soil and remained intimate with their pagan past, heirs to an ancient folkloric tradition of depth, richness and diversity.

St Vladimir

St Vladimir, revered as the man who brought Christianity to the first Russian state, was a warring prince and not the gentle contemplative his canonization might suggest.

Vladimir was born in 956 in Kiev, son of Svyatoslav and one of his many courtesans. He became prince of Novgorod in 970, but when his father was slaughtered by Pechenegs in 972, the young prince fled to Scandinavia. He later returned, however, and was soon to be crowned as Grand Prince of Kievan Rus.

Famous for high living and low morals, Vladimir had seven wives and, according to some accounts, as many as 1,000 concubines. He also established pagan temples and took part in human sacrifices to Perun, the thunder god (see page 36). His conversion to Christianity was linked to a request for military aid by Byzantium's Emperor Basil II (976–1025). As part of the deal, Vladimir was offered the hand of the emperor's daughter in marriage. He agreed to be baptized.

According to Nestor's *Primary Chronicle*, on returning to Kiev after a successful campaign, Vladimir commanded that all pagan idols be hurled into the Dnieper River (see page 43). He was later canonized and became a great folk hero, the subject of countless *byliny*, or folk epics.

Notables welcome Vladimir back to Kiev as a conquering hero and a Christian, from an ancient banner. St Vladimir is also credited with establishing Russia as the natural heir to the Byzantine Empire.

THE PEOPLE'S ART

The elaborate designs and colourful images of Russian folk art obscure the tradition's practical origins. Villages isolated amid the forests and steppes of eastern Europe had to be self-sufficient. Clothes and tools, therefore, would all be made from local materials and then embellished with motifs which were either symbols of spiritual protection or marks of status and ownership. Designs changed little until the 1800s when Russia's urban elite began to tire of the European fashions that had been popular since the reign of Peter the Great. Craftsmen were introduced to factory-style work to meet the demand for more indigenous art forms but, by serving the customer rather than the maker, folk art gradually became stylized and distanced from its roots. It remains, however, an essential expression of Slavic cultural identity.

Below: **Magical symbols adorn the walls of a Polish farmhouse. Motifs that were imbued with protective powers – of the Tree of Life, the mother goddess and various birds and beasts – were also used to decorate clothes and tools. The designs were taken from an inherited pool of symbols and reflected the consciousness of the community rather than the individual vision of a particular artist.**

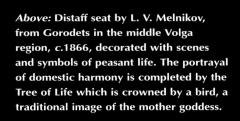

Above: **Distaff seat by L. V. Melnikov, from Gorodets in the middle Volga region, c.1866, decorated with scenes and symbols of peasant life. The portrayal of domestic harmony is completed by the Tree of Life which is crowned by a bird, a traditional image of the mother goddess.**

Left: Late 19th-century painted distaff comb, used for spinning wool by hand, also from Gorodets in the middle Volga. The images which decorate the comb celebrate the domestic life of the peasant woman for whom the arts of spinning and weaving were central activities.

Above: Matreshka dolls, perhaps the best-known product of Russian folk art, were first made in the 1890s for purely commercial purposes. The dolls capture a playful aspect of the Russian imagination reflected in many fairytales in which the object of a hero's quest may be found in a box which lies inside a duck within a hare which was itself hidden in the belly of another, larger animal (see pages 100–101).

Left: The intricate patterns and bright colours on this dyed skirt from the Czech Republic, 20th century, would not have served simply as decoration. Traditionally, colour and pattern reflected aspects of social tradition and personal status. The motifs would be handed down from mother to daughter, and even if they lost their original meaning, they would retain a local significance – by showing, for example, whether the wearer was married.

PANTHEON OF THE SLAVS

In the early twentieth century, peasants deep in the Russian countryside still practised an archaic ritual of earth magic handed down by their ancestors from pagan times. When an epidemic of cattle or human sickness hit a village, the women set out at midnight to perform *opakhivanie* ("ploughing around"). In the darkness of the fields they stripped to their underwear and shook their hair free. Some hauled the plough, others raised a fearsome racket by howling and banging sticks and pans. They circled the entire village, digging a magic furrow that released the healing power of Mother Earth to combat the evil responsible for the illness.

For centuries after officially becoming Christians, peasants in Russia and many other Slavic countries remained intimate with the pagan rites of their forebears. Scholars who investigated Slavic folk beliefs in the nineteenth century were astounded by the extent to which the peasants, while practising Orthodox Christianity, were still connected to their pagan inheritance. The phenomenon became known as *dvoeverie*, or "dual faith".

Below: **Stone circles, like this one in Hungary, were the focus of pagan worship. The Slavs also favoured wooded sites and hilltops.**

It is not clear, however, what the religious life of pagan Slavs was like before the conversion to Christianity. Evidence collected by folklorists in the nineteenth century suggests that the Slavs' primary cults were of the fertile Mother Earth and of their ancestors. They may also have worshipped elemental forces such as fire, air and water and performed rites in the open countryside on hilltops, at the foot of sacred trees or in forest clearings. The various contemporary sources, however, suggest that the chief gods of the pagan Slavs were warrior and sky deities.

But these ancient accounts may only give half the picture. The chronicles were compiled by a political elite largely based in towns. The deities described may have been relatively new gods even when they were overthrown by Christianity, and their cult may also have been heavily influenced by contact with non-Slavs such as the Varangian princes from Scandinavia who some scholars say were instrumental in the establishment of Kievan Rus. Out in the isolated country villages, the people may well have followed older ways, revering their forebears, the life-giving sun and the sacred earth, and after the collapse of state paganism and the coming of Christianity, they continued to practise their own rites in honour of the ancient deities.

Opposite: **Identifying the exact significance of particular ancient gods is highly problematic. This central European deity dates from the 4th–3rd millennium BC. It carries a sickle, a symbol of both fertility and death, but how it was worshipped remains a mystery.**

The Forces of Night and Day

According to Helmold's *Chronicle of the Slavs, c.*1170, the tribes of the Baltic region prayed both to a good and a bad god. Success and well-being were the gifts of the benign deity while evil fortune was sent by the bad.

Helmold referred to a deity named Chernobog ("Black God") who was worshipped by the Baltic Slavs – and according to some historians his cult was matched by that of Belobog ("White God"). This theory maintains that Belobog, god of light and the sky, was in constant conflict with Chernobog, god of darkness and the earth. The evidence is uncertain, however, and other writers insist that Belobog is no more than the product of scholars' elaborate fantasy.

Yet Belun, a familiar figure of Belorussian legend, may have been a descendant of this mysterious white god. Belun was a tall, frail old man with a streaming white beard who dressed in flowing white robes and carried a long staff. When a weary traveller was lost and frightened in the thick forest he would often encounter the kindly old man, who would lead him out into the bright sunlight. At harvest Belun sometimes walked into the fields alone to help the peasants in their labours. He would only appear in daylight hours.

In many Russian folktales describing the creation of the universe, a bright celestial spirit of good has to struggle with a dark earthly spirit of evil. One such tale reveals that at the beginning of time God ruled in Heaven over a realm of light while the Earth was a kingdom of darkness governed by Tsar Santanail.

Santanail made people from clay, but he could not bring them to life and had to watch with sour envy as God gave them souls and took them to Heaven. Eventually, heavy with dark thoughts, he decided to make his way there himself, drawn towards its brilliant light. He could not go in but, perched on the very rim of paradise, succeeded in tempting the first people back to Earth. Then God in righteous indignation created a shining army of celestial warriors. Tsar Santanail immediately countered with a force of dark demons and the two armies fought in the sky for the magical number of seventy-seven days until the forces of light finally won. The bright lord left the first people on Earth, teaching them about good and evil. He then hung his burning sword in the sky in the form of the sun. While it shone Santanail and his demons had to hide, but at night when the sun went down the forces of evil ran riot.

Lightning – the Gaze of the Gods

The flash of lightning that seems to set night or day on fire was seen as the sudden glance of a great giant in many Slavic countries. It could be a sign of anger or even of playfulness.

The Serbians told of a dread giant named Vii, whose fierce gaze burned men or even whole villages to dust. His eyes were usually closed and hidden behind thick brows, but from time to time his assistants lifted the brows and forced back the eyelids, using great pitchforks. Then his bright eyes blazed forth for a terrible, destructive instant.

Russian peasants told similar stories of a giant with fiery eyes hidden behind thick eyelashes and lids that were sometimes pulled apart by attendants. In the Christian tradition they became associated with the baleful St Cassian, "the Unmerciful". Cassian was said to sit on a chair, his eyes hidden behind brows so overgrown that they reached his knees. Once every four years, on his feast day of 29 February, he threw back his head and lifted his brows to look at the world created by the good God. He brought plague and death wherever he looked.

The Bohemians and Slovaks spoke of a giant called Swifteye, whose glance could start a blazing fire. He wore a bandage over his eyes, but when the weather was wild and the thunder was shaking the Earth the cloth sometimes slipped, unveiling his fiery gaze. Another more light-hearted tradition, common in parts of Russia, held that the lightning flashed because a great giant had playfully winked. They called the summer lightning Morgavka – from the Russian *morgat*, to wink – and when storms swept the sky they called on the giant to wink.

Amid the vast eastern European plains, thunder and lightning were a constant, angry presence and the source of several myths. Many Slavs feared such phenomena as the wrath of gods. Some Russians, however, believed that the fearsome flashes came from a giant who had playfully winked.

Belief in "dualism" – that good and evil powers forever dispute the universe – probably came from the Middle East. Linguistic evidence suggests that the ancestors of the first Slavs were influenced religiously by the Scythians and the Sarmatians, nomads from Persia. The Slavic word *raj* ("Paradise") is derived from the Persian *ray* ("Heavenly Light") while the Slavic sky god Svarog takes the -og suffix from Persian.

Dualistic beliefs resurfaced in tenth-century Bulgaria when a priest named Bogomil began preaching the ideas of the Persian prophet Mani. The Russian *Primary Chronicle* described the interrogation of two priests who subscribed to his heretical views. They said that the human body was the work of the Devil, but that God gave men and women souls; at death the body would go to the earth whereas the soul would fly to God.

31

Deities of the Baltic Slavs

Slavic tribes living on the shores of the Baltic Sea worshipped towering carved images of war and nature gods housed in magnificent temples. Near-contemporary accounts and archaeological evidence provide a picture of the pagan rites practised by these early Slavs.

A temple to the war god Svantovit ("Strong Lord") stood on the island of Rügen, off the coast near Rostock in what is now eastern Germany. On a clifftop high above the pounding waves of the Baltic – according to Saxo Grammaticus, the twelfth-century Danish chronicler – the god's four-headed wooden statue stood in a temple inside the castle of Arcona. The shrine's outer walls were decorated with paintings and carvings and topped with a red roof; in the inner precinct four pillars supported the roof and thick purple cloths took the place of walls. Svantovit's four heads looked in the cardinal directions.

The statue's right hand held a drinking horn of precious metal, used by a priest for a fortune-telling rite each year; the left arm was folded a little way beneath the right as if placed across the god's stomach. A saddle, a bridle and a splendidly decorated sword hung beside it. Svantovit's main festival was at harvest time: he was a god of fertility and protector of crops as well as a war deity. Some scholars argue that he was worshipped as a supreme god, above all others.

In the harvest festival the chief priest presented Svantovit with a large loaf of honey bread and poured wine into the statue's drinking horn; later in the ceremonies he examined the wine to see if any had disappeared. If little or no wine had gone, it was a good omen – but if much had been taken by the god then the next year's harvest would be poor and the priest would instruct the people to prepare for a lean year.

The shores of Rügen Island, the site of some of the earliest known Slavic temples. Unlike most holy places, which were simple forest clearings or hilltops, the shrines to the ancient gods here were built in stone.

A white horse dedicated to Svantovit was kept in the temple and treated with the utmost reverence. The warriors of Rügen believed that the god himself rode into battle with them astride this proud steed. If he brought them victory, then they offered him one-third of their booty. A force of 300 mounted warriors was dedicated to the god's service. But the historical record reveals that Svantovit was unable to help the Slavs against the Danish invasion of 1168; his temple at Arcona was razed to the ground and his statue burned on the orders of the Danish king, Valdemar.

Svantovit's white horse played the central role in another fortune-telling rite. Before the armies set out for war the priest laid spears criss-cross on the ground and sent the horse forward. If the sacred animal passed over them easily, then all would be well; but if it stumbled, catching its feet – or in some accounts, if it led with its left foot – than it was a bad omen and the military expedition might even be called off.

Gods with Many Faces

Other gods of these early Slavs were, like Svantovit, fierce and warlike but they too probably had fertility aspects connecting them to the seasons and life in the fields. At Gardziec – now known as Gartz, also on Rügen – stood a temple to Rugievit or Ruievit. His great idol stood in an inner temple like that of Svantovit with a roof supported by pillars between which were purple hangings. Carved from oak, the statue of Rugievit had seven faces and carried seven swords slung from its girdle while in its right hand it held an eighth. According to Saxo Grammaticus, Rugievit's name meant "God of Rügen".

Another god worshipped on Rügen and mentioned by Saxo Grammaticus was Porevit but little is known of his cult save that it may have been connected to midsummer rites. Rugievit's temple and shrines dedicated to Porevit and Porenut were also destroyed by the Danish troops in 1168.

The stern Yarovit had a great golden shield in his temple, and it was carried out with banners before going into battle. Sites associated with the god have been excavated at Wolgast (on the Baltic coast of eastern Germany) and Havelberg (northeast of Berlin). The temple at Wolgast was destroyed in 1128 during a Christian mission led by Bishop Otto of Bamberg; his men entered the temple and discovered the golden shield, which they carried outside. An angry crowd had gathered, but when they saw the shield they fell down in awe, believing that the great god himself had descended to Earth. Yarovit was connected to spring and was believed to have power over the fertility of fields.

Another hilltop temple – at Riedegost, now Rethra (eastern Germany) – was described by Thietmar, Bishop of Merseburg, in 1014. Its timber walls were decorated with animal horns and sculptures, and it housed a number of wooden idols dressed in battle armour. The chief of these was,

Svantovit was worshipped in the form of a white horse which would ride into battle alongside the warriors of Rügen. Warlike images permeate Slavic art, providing themes for epic poetry and motifs for embroidery, like this 19th-century lace towel.

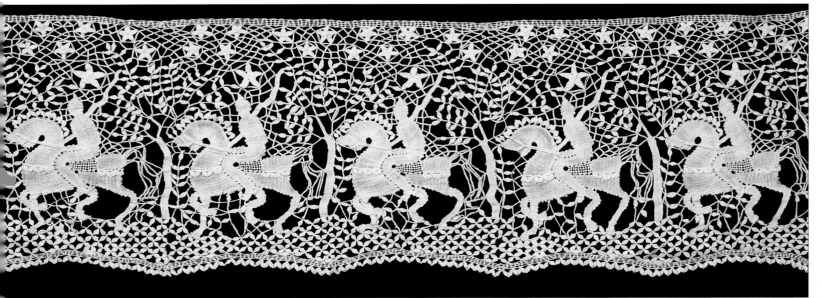

A Hero from the Holy Mountains

The epic hero, or bogatyr, *Svyatogor met his match when he least expected it. His tale comes from one of the earliest extant cycles of* byliny, *or songs, celebrating the mythical "Elder heroes".*

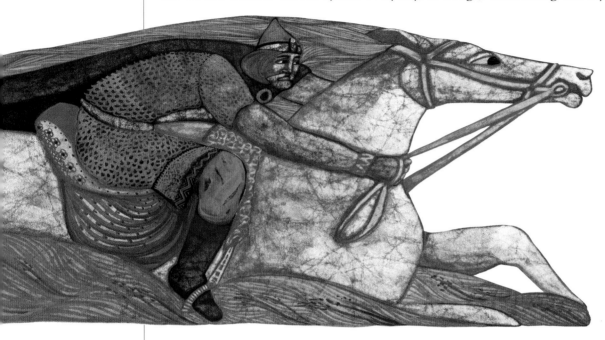

Svyatogor was a warrior of peerless strength and courage. When peasants looked up to see him pounding the plains on his tall horse they saw a fearless warrior, a leader of men – almost a god. He took his name from his home – in Russian *V Svyatykh Gorakh* ("Among the Holy Mountains").

One day Svyatogor prepared to set out on a long journey across the steppes. He whistled a familiar tune and stroked his powerful steed as he strapped on his favourite saddle, which was decorated with jewels and silken threads. Then he leaped up and set off at a gallop.

Svyatogor would ride across the steppes upon his mighty steed, admired by all who saw him. The smallest of things, however, proved his undoing.

On the plains the sun was warm and the wind swept briskly over the long grasses. Svyatogor felt full of life. Far away he spotted a wild boar and clenched his hands on the reins, feeling the power of his own strength – so great that it was like a weight he carried around. He laughed as he looked across the immense plain and shouted a boast that he was strong enough to lift the entire Earth in his bare hands.

Then he saw a saddle bag on the ground before him. Curious, the great warrior brought his horse to a standstill and tried to flick the bag up with his whip handle: but it would not move. Next he leaned down and attempted to raise it with his finger: but it was as heavy as a boulder. Still in the saddle, he tried to shift the bag with one hand, without success. Again Svyatogor laughed, for he realized the bag was enchanted and that meant a challenge.

Down he leaped and took the sack with both hands. Roaring with the effort, he succeeded in lifting the bag to the level of his knees. But when he looked down he saw that he had sunk deep into the earth and that the bag still rested on the ground. Red drops splashed onto his arms – for tears of blood were pouring from his eyes.

Svyatogor tried to clamber out but he was trapped, held magically by the clinging soil. Now he howled with rage, and yelled for help. But he was in the midst of the great plain, far from any settlement. He saw a group of wild horses gallop past and after a while his own faithful horse abandoned him. The great *bogatyr* bitterly regretted his boast. And there in that lonely place, the great man met his untimely end, slowly wasting away under the unheeding sky.

he said, Zuarasici – interpreted by scholars as a version of Svarozhich, god of fire among the East Slavs. The bishop reported that troops worshipped in the temple before going to war and brought offerings to the god on their safe return. The temple priest cast horse-bone oracles and dice to determine what form the offerings should take.

Archaeologists have established that the temple was erected in around AD1000 and appears to have been burned to the ground in 1068. Other written sources suggest that a god named Radogost – which scholars suggest is a mistaken application of the place-name Riedegost to Svarozhich – was worshipped in this temple.

This ancient stone statue of a pagan god, found on the Baltic island of Rügen, is believed to represent Svantovit. The god was often depicted with a drinking horn in his hand. He was a god of fertility as well as of war.

A three-headed god named Triglav was worshipped by the Slavs of Pomerania. He was celebrated as a supreme deity, and is thought by some scholars to be another name for the sky god Svarog worshipped in eastern Slav lands. Herbordus, a scholar who wrote one of three biographies of Bishop Otto of Bamberg, described a temple built to Triglav at Stettin (in Poland), which he said housed sculptures of animals, birds and people so lifelike that a visitor would mistake them for living creatures. When Otto visited the temple in around 1124, he commanded that Triglav's three heads be chopped off and dispatched to Pope Callixtus II. Other images of Triglav stood at Brandenburg (west of Berlin) and as far away as Skradin (on the Adriatic coast of Croatia). Triglav's three heads must have represented his wide dominion, for his followers believed that he ruled over sky, Earth and underworld; he wore blindfolds like the thunder giants of folklore, but in his case because he did not wish to witness the evil done by men and women.

Other archaeological finds have established that the early western Slavs' temples and idols were generally made of wood and usually built on high ground, within the ramparts of a hill fort. Worshippers made offerings of acorns, tiny replicas of bread and grains made from clay – and even of cooking pots.

The cult of Svantovit casts an intriguing light on finds of idols in other parts of the Slav lands. Stone statues – many with three or four heads and holding a drinking horn – have been unearthed in the upper reaches of the Dniester River in Poland, dating from around the fourth century AD. Some wear pointed caps and are decorated with carved symbols of horses and suns. A celebrated stone statue almost three metres tall was found in the River Zbrucz in Galicia, southeastern Poland, in 1848. It had four heads and was claimed at the time to be an image of Svantovit since it held the drinking horn associated with that god. Recently, however, some historians have suggested it may not have been Slavic at all but rather a relic left in the area by Turkish nomads in the Middle Ages.

The Pagan Gods of Kiev

In the late tenth century a cluster of pagan idols stood on a hillside above Kiev. Tradition has it that human sacrifices were made to these gods with Prince Vladimir's backing. But before his reign was out the statues were denounced and pitched into the Dnieper River.

When Vladimir took power in Kievan Rus in around 980, he erected idols to six pagan gods, according to the Russian *Primary Chronicle*. They towered against the sky on the open hillside, where worshippers felt the full power of nature in the heat of the sun, the buffeting of the wind or the thunder of an approaching storm. The chronicle also reveals that the land was drenched in human blood as the pagan Russians devotedly brought their sons and daughters to sacrifice to the gods. But the account, by Christian monks, is certainly exaggerated and may have been entirely fabricated; historians have noted that the passage is little more than a paraphrase of part of Psalm 106 in the Bible, which describes the wickedness of apostate Jews in worshipping pagan idols with the Canaanites. It remains true, however, that human sacrifice was known among Slavic pagans.

The chronicle also recounts that Vladimir installed his uncle Dobrynya to rule at Novgorod, and Dobrynya ordered an idol of Perun to be built there, on the banks of the Volkhov River. The

The Carpenter, Perun and the Devil

In a folktale of the Christian era, Perun and the Devil became the companions of a humble carpenter.

The wide plains and dark, forbidding forests of Russia held no fear for the three unusual travellers. Perun relied on his thunderbolts to drive back predatory beasts and the Devil used all his wiles to capture animals for their supper. The skilful carpenter would then cook the hunting spoils.

The three found a place to live in the forest, and the carpenter built a hut. Between them they began to grow vegetables until, one night, a thief came and stole all their turnips.

Perun was furious and the following night lay in wait for the robber, thunderbolts in hand. He heard the creak of wagon wheels and flung himself into the darkness, but he was caught by a stinging whip and brought to his knees. Hearing the sorry tale next day, the Devil laughed and promised to gain revenge. But on the following night he too was thrashed by the mysterious miscreant.

The third night came, and the carpenter sat up, armed only with a violin. At midnight he began to play a folk dance. Instantly the thief appeared, a withered old woman, who begged to be taught the tune.

The carpenter promised the old hag that he could transform her old fingers into supple ones, capable of mastering the notes. Leading her to a tree that he had split with an axe, he persuaded her to place her hands in the crack, then quickly knocked the wedge away, trapping her fingers. The witch wailed and begged to be freed. He made her promise never to return to the hut and then drove her away in her cart, which he subsequently kept for his own use.

remains of an outdoor shrine, which may have been dedicated to Perun, were excavated in 1951, four kilometres south of the city of Peryn. Archaeologists found a central mound surrounded by a ditch now filled with charcoal, which led them to speculate that an idol had once stood there surrounded by sacred fires.

The chronicler identified six gods in Vladimir's pagan pantheon, the foremost of which was Perun, god of thunder and war. The majestic statue of Perun in Kiev had a wooden body with a silver head and a golden moustache. He may have been worshipped as the supreme god. Procopius, the sixth-century Byzantine historian, wrote that the East Slavs worshipped the god of the thunderbolt as Lord of the Universe and sacrificed animals including oxen, bears and goats to win his favour.

As god of war, Perun carried a battle-axe, a spear and a club, and held in his favour the balance of success or failure in war. Accordingly, Slavic warriors swore oaths on his name both before and after battle: the *Primary Chronicle* tells how, when Prince Igor made a treaty with Byzantium in 945, he and his

Perun, the Devil and the carpenter decided to part soon afterwards. All three wanted to remain in the hut so they agreed to hold a contest, with the prize going to the one who was able to frighten the other two. The Devil went first, whipping up a raging wind. Perun fled, but the carpenter put his faith in God and stayed. The next night Perun unleashed a deafening thunderstorm. This time the Devil decamped, but the carpenter sat calmly through it.

When it was his turn, the carpenter crept away to fetch the witch's wagon and rode up to the house at midnight, taunting the others with their failures. The Devil and Perun fled the hut, never to return – and the carpenter settled down to a happy life on his own.

While the Devil fled when Perun summoned up his thunderbolts and Perun could not endure the storm conjured by the Devil, the carpenter remained calm, praying quietly to his God. He then took up the task himself and forced the other two to flee in fear.

37

Icon of the fiery ascent to Heaven of Ilya or Elijah, with scenes from his life, by Ignati Panteleev, from Russia c.1647. Thunder was held to herald Elijah riding across the sky, aligning the prophet with the ancient storm god Perun.

warriors laid their weapons and shields before a statue of Perun and pledged to honour the agreement.

In Russian folk tradition, Perun was an awesome figure with the build of a powerful warrior, a head of thick black hair and a cascading golden beard. He took to the skies in a chariot bright with flames, carrying a burning bow in one hand and a quiver of arrows in the other. When he was angry he unleashed lightning bolts to strike down his enemies. In some accounts he rode on a millstone carried by his servants, the spirits of the mountains, and their flight set loose the flash of lightning and crack of thunder across the echoing sky.

The oak tree, often struck by lightning, was held sacred to Perun. Farmers needed to placate him, for he might destroy a year's crops with a blast of drought or a sweep of hail; but equally he had it in his power to send gentle, life-giving rains to water the fields. He was Lord of the Harvest.

Slavic peasants commonly believed that the first thunderstorm of the spring brought the earth back to life in a rush of green grass and leaves after the death of winter. Thunder and lightning were life-giving forces: according to Slavic folklore, people or trees who had been struck by lightning had the power to bring good health. After the coming of Christianity – when Perun had been assimilated into the Biblical image of the chariot-riding prophet Ilya (Elijah) – Russian peasants believed that during a thunderstorm Ilya chased devils across heaven.

When the early Russians found belemnites – mollusc fossils that look a little like arrowheads – they handled them with awe as the very thunderbolts that Perun had flung in his rage from on high. The peasants believed that Perun's bolts penetrated deep into the earth, where they stayed for a magic period – usually three or seven years – before rising to the surface. They used these fossils as icons – for protection against storms, for good fortune or to bring back the flow of milk to cows that had dried up. Sometimes the rainbow was associated with the great bow of Perun. The god's name survived as a Slavic word for thunder, and in popular curses – such as one used by Russians and Slovenians, "May Perun take you!"

The Glittering Sun

The other gods identified by the chronicler in Vladimir's pagan pantheon were Khors, Dazhbog, Stribog, Simargl and Mokosh. Dazhbog was a sun god, offspring of a great sky deity named Svarog. According to a work by the sixth-century Byzantine chronicler John Malala, Svarog had two sons, the sun – Dazhbog – and fire – Svarozhich ("Son of Svarog"). Scholars believe that Khors was probably an aspect of Dazhbog or else simply another name for him. Svarog – not named in the

Perun's Flowers

Croatians said fern flowers flourished only for a few hours once or twice a year. They called the blooms Perenovo Tsvetje *– the flowers of Perun – and credited them with mystical powers.*

Although ferns do not, strictly speaking, flower, one particular species, called *Osmunda regalis*, sprouts colourful fronds. The rarity of these blooms and their striking golden-red colour have been the subject of much folklore – for according to some cultures these were blossoms that could unlock the very secrets of the universe. When the plant flowered, so legends claimed, demons used thunderstorms and magic spells to guard it for their own use. But whoever succeeded in gathering the blooms in spite of their efforts gained the power to fulfil all their desires.

The oldest tradition linked the flower to the pagan festival of Kupala when sacred waters, plants and trees were venerated (see page 45). Kupala was closely associated with the summer solstice and after the coming of Christianity was celebrated with the Church festival of St John the Baptist on 24 June.

Peasants believed that the golden, fire-like bloom of the fern appeared at midnight on Kupala night and shone so brightly that human eyes could not bear to look at it directly. A man or woman brave or rash enough to try to gather it had to venture into the forest that evening – and wait. They had to draw a magic circle around the plant and stand within it. All around them demons would caper and shout, calling their name; if they answered or stepped out of the circle they would be ripped apart. They must remain patiently without fear while the forest moved and mingled around them – for on that night the very trees had the power to raise their roots, walk and talk. In the instant the flower appeared, they had to seize it. Then they would be safe, for the flower could defeat demons, bring prosperity or success in love, unlock the secrets of buried treasure – and even enable people to understand the language of the trees.

In the Christian era another tradition held that the flower bloomed on Easter eve. A man or woman wanting to pick the flower had to bring with them a cloth on which an Easter cake had been blessed in Church and the knife with which the holy cake had been cut. In the forest they had to draw a circle around the fern with the knife and sit inside the circle on the cloth. While they waited for the fern to blossom, demons would unleash terrifying thunderstorms or mutter insidious spells that had the power to plunge the unwary into a dreamless sleep. But at the moment when in churches near and far worshippers declared triumphantly that Christ was risen and had defeated death, the fern would flower. Then the seeker had to take the bloom, throw the cloth over their head and shoulders and flee the forest without looking behind them. Safely home, they should use the knife to cut their hand and dress the wound with the herb. Then at last the flower's magic would be unleashed and all secrets unveiled.

The golden-red flowers of the flowering fern, *Osmunda regalis*, were linked to holy figures such as Perun and Ivan Kupala. The blooms were regarded as sacred and could offer powerful gifts to those who managed to pick them.

Primary Chronicle's pantheon – was creator and supreme god. He was identified with Hephaestus, the divine smith of the Greeks. He ruled the entire universe, but there came a time when he chose to transfer authority to his sons. Dazhbog was also revered as a source of wealth and good things, for peasants imagined the sun god as a just and honourable ruler, and as avenger of wrongs. A number of peasant curses called on the sun to bring ruin to an enemy.

Slavic tribes revered both the sun and the domestic hearth fire as sacred. By tradition, younger members of the household had to observe silence when the hearth fire was lit. No one would spit in the fire or be less than respectful towards it. Russians – accustomed to warming their cold, aching bodies before the hearth in the winter – believed that flames could drive away sickness. When an epidemic struck down the cattle herd, the cows were driven through bonfires lit from a holy fire made by spinning a peg in round holes that had been drilled in a block of wood.

There is strong evidence that the Slavs worshipped the sun from ancient times. Ceramic remains from Lusatia dated to 1700BC bear symbols suggesting a solar cult. Much later, Al-Masudi, an Arab traveller to Slavic lands in the tenth century, described a temple constructed for observing the sunrise. Russians believed solar eclipses were evil portents, presaging epidemic or famine; the episode of darkness occurred because the sun had been caught and devoured by scavenging wolves. Traditional prayers to the sun have been collected in Poland and Ukraine.

Many folk traditions concerning the sun grew up among Slavic peoples. The Serbs said he was a youthful king who ruled from a throne of purple and gold over a land bathed in glorious light. His uncle, bald in his old age, was Mesyats (the moon). Also in his retinue were the fair maidens of Dawn and Dusk, seven stern judges – the planets – and seven fleet celestial messengers, comets whose long tails streamed out after them as they crossed the heavens. Other traditions told how each morning the sun left his glittering palace in the east to ride the sky in a fiery chariot; according to the Poles his car was made from diamonds and pulled by a team of twelve golden-maned horses with coats of purest white. Some legends held that each day was a solar lifetime, with the sun born anew every dawn, growing to adulthood in the morning, then in the afternoon declining to

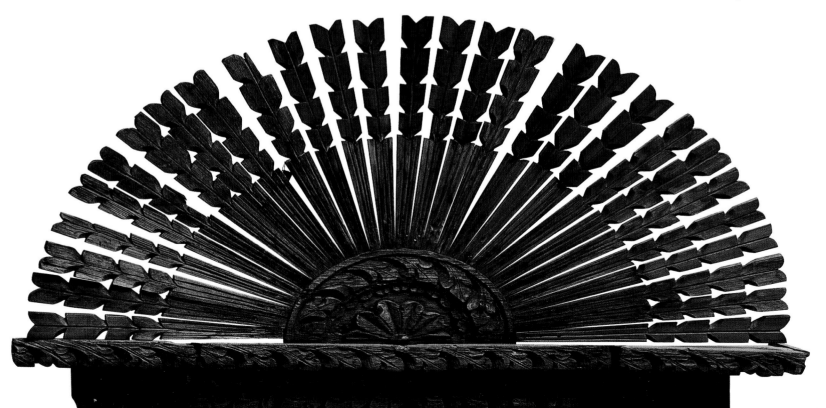

An embroidered Russian towel, *c.*19th century, showing a double-headed eagle flanked by symbols of the mother goddess with her arms in the air. Some scholars believe that the Slavs' ancient veneration of the eagle may be linked to the Persian worship of the griffin whose divine form, Simourg, may have been the original influence for the Slavic god Simargl.

Opposite: **There is strong evidence that the Slavs worshipped the sun from the very earliest times and it is still venerated today. This late 19th-century solar symbol once crowned the window frame of a Russian cottage in the Volga region.**

old age and eventual death at dusk. Another poetic interpretation, found among the Russians, saw sun and moon as husband and wife. In spring the sun wooed the delicate, pale-complexioned moon and they were married amid much rejoicing at the start of summer. Their many children were the stars. When they argued, the Earth trembled, causing earthquakes. In winter the sun left his wife, causing much suffering on Earth, but with the coming of spring the errant sun happily returned. Often, however, the moon was considered to be male; the name Mesyats in Russian is masculine. A Ukrainian tradition depicted the moon as the husband and the sun as his wife.

Scholars have established that Svarog, Svarozhich and Dazhbog were the only gods known to all Slavic peoples. Baltic Slavs worshipped Zuarasici (a version of Svarozhich's name) at Riedegost, in eastern Germany (see page 35). Some have argued that several of the Slavic gods known to history were aspects of a great sun god worshipped by prehistoric Slavs or even the Indo-Europeans who in the third millennium BC were moving across lands later occupied by the Slavs. The derivation of Svarog's name may be linked to *svarga*, the word for sky or sun in Sanskrit, the Indian language derived from that of the Indo-European nomads.

Deities of Wind and Rain

Of the other gods listed in the *Primary Chronicle*, almost nothing is known about Simargl; some scholars link the name to the Persian Simourg, a divine griffin – a lion with eagle's head, wings and claws – who was protector of green shoots and seeds; Slavic tribes may have adopted the god from the Sarmatians who worshipped the deity under the name Simarg. The cult of the winged god may have resonated with an existing Slavic reverence for the eagle; by folk tradition in Serbia, Bosnia and Bulgaria, the eagle dispatched hailstorms over the plain and when crossed could be devastating, unleashing fire or sickness as punishment. In some manuscripts two gods, Sim and Regl, are listed. Some scholars suggest that the name Simargl was invented by the chronicler.

Little more is known about Stribog, the East Slavs' god of winds. *The Lay of Igor's Campaign*, a twelfth-century poem, however, suggests that the winds were his grandchildren.

The final deity, Mokosh ("Moist"), may be a survival of an ancient cult of the fertility goddess. She had power over life-giving waters – when drought threatened, Czech peasants prayed to Mokosh for rain – and may be a personification of the "Moist Mother Earth" revered by Russians (see page 54). Scholars believe that images in Russian embroidery of a woman with raised hands flanked by mounted attendants – still commonly made at the end of the nineteenth century – are of Mokosh. She later became associated with women's work, such as washing and spinning. Women made offerings to her in the belief she would help them with their laundry. Even in the twentieth century, Russian peasants told of a female spirit named Mokusha who appeared at night to spin wool, or

sometimes stole the wool from the very backs of the sheep during the hours of darkness. Strands of wool were left out for her as offerings.

God of Cattle and Oaths

Volos, god of cattle, was a significant old Slavic god whose name was not included in the *Primary Chronicle*'s list of idols. His exact status is not known. He may at one time have been primarily a god of the peasants, and so have had an uncertain place in the princely pantheon of Kiev – but he became associated with Perun and clearly was a deity revered by warriors. When Prince Svyatoslav made a treaty with Byzantium in 971 he and his soldiers swore on their swords both by Perun and by Volos to keep their side of the agreement. Volos has also been identified as a prehistoric god of flocks and forests with authority over dead beasts and the wild animals hunted by the earliest tribesmen on the Russian plains, but there is little evidence to support this theory.

Only in Kievan Rus and on the Baltic coast did the early Slavs worship a developed pantheon of pagan gods – and these were the areas where they came into close contact with Scandinavian adventurers. The Baltic Slavs were harassed by Gothic raiders from the west and Finnish and Scandinavian boatmen from the north, while the early Russians lived side by side with the Varangian princes who may have played a significant role in the creation of Kievan Rus. Some

scholars argue that the pagan gods of the Baltic and Kievan Slavs were derived from the warrior gods of the Scandinavians.

The cult of Perun, for instance, may have been influenced by that of the Norse god Thor. Like Perun, Thor was god of thunder, storms and fertility; and like Igor and his troops, Scandinavian warriors used to lay their weapons before statues of him. However, Thor was never worshipped as the supreme god, for that place in the Norse pantheon was taken by Odin. Scholars have established a link between the name Perun and the Norse Jord, Thor's mother, who was perhaps a survival of an ancient fertility goddess.

In the nineteenth century there was a fashion among scholars of the "mythological school" to trace links between European mythologies and the beliefs of the early Indo-European nomads. In this period Perun was compared to Parjanja, an aspect of the war god Indra, and Volos with the Aryan god Varuna, who was associated with cattle. While the descriptions of these gods may bear distinct similarities, today such comparisons are seen, at best, as fanciful.

Idols Cast Down

When Prince Vladimir converted to Christianity in 988 he ordered the destruction of the idols he had erected just eight years previously. According to the *Primary Chronicle*, Perun's statue was knocked down, tied to a horse and dragged through mud to the river. Soldiers battered it with sticks before dispatching it into the Dnieper. The god's devotees wept as his image was dishonoured. Once in the water, Perun was carried downstream by the current but then beached on the bank; the area where it stuck became known as "Perun's Bank". The thunder god's idol in Novgorod was also hauled down, and thrown into the river, but he lived on in folk memory. Even in the twentieth century, the inhabitants of Novgorod were known to cast a coin into the river when passing the spot where Perun's image once stood.

43

A Dual Faith

When Prince Vladimir dismantled the pantheon of pagan gods and imposed Christianity on Kievan Rus in 988, the Russians appear to have put up little resistance. Yet despite their conversion to Christianity, many people continued to practise the ancient pagan rites.

A late 15th-century icon of John the Baptist. As well as inheriting the attributes of the pagan fertility figure Ivan Kupala, John, who was beheaded by King Herod, also became linked, ironically, with the relief of headaches.

The Slavic peasants still believed in the power of the natural forces their ancestors had once worshipped as pagan gods, but now revered them in the guise of Christian saints. They were not deliberately hiding paganism beneath a veneer of Orthodox respectability, for they saw themselves as good Christians. The coexistence of pagan custom and Christianity, usually described as *dvoeverie* or "dual faith", has been identified mostly in studies of Russia but is a phenomenon that also applies to peasants in other Slavic countries, particularly those within the Orthodox Church.

Up to the nineteenth and twentieth centuries the Slavic peasant farmer remained dependent on the fertility of the land and largely isolated from change. Folkloric customs persisted alongside Christianity in other cultures too – but not to the same extent, for most of the Slavic world did not experience the upheavals of the Renaissance or the Reformation. Some scholars who investigated Russian folk belief in the nineteenth century went so far as to claim that the peasants were still effectively pagans; others, however, believed them to be infused with a deep spirituality and reverence for the God and saints of the Orthodox Church.

For the first few hundred years after the conversion of Russia, Christianity was largely confined to the princely elite, and many parts of the country remained virtually untouched by the new faith – at least until the Mongol invasion of the thirteenth century, when Orthodox Christianity became a shared symbol of Russian identity. Even after this, however, the Orthodox Church was not well represented in the Russian countryside, for the country clergy were poor, ill-educated, often prone to drunkenness and treated with derision by the people. The Church hierarchy tried to stamp out pre-Christian rituals but with little success.

Clean and Unclean Forces

The Russian peasants had a strong belief in a malign influence they called the *nechistaya sila* ("unclean force"). They used the term to refer to the Devil of Christianity as well as to malign nature spirits of the old pagan ways. The unclean force was responsible for all kinds of evil or bad luck, from minor upsets like a headache to serious illness or crop failure. For help against this force the peasants appealed to the saints. St John the Baptist, for instance, could cure headaches, while St Catherine the Martyr could save women from a

Pagan Feasts and Christian Festivals

The fertility festivals of the Slav peasants followed the rhythm of the agricultural year. They were largely assimilated into the Orthodox Church's calendar of feast days. The great majority of the old rites practised at pagan festivals thus survived the coming of the new religion.

The midwinter pagan festival of Yuletide, tied to the winter solstice, was celebrated alongside the Church festivals of Christmas and Epiphany. Peasants held masked processions and mock funerals in which a person pretending to be dead – or sometimes an actual corpse – was carried around and mourned amid great hilarity. A Yuletide food – a grain porridge named *kutya* – became a traditional part of the spread on Christmas Eve.

Spring ceremonies of Shrovetide became the pre-Lenten festival of carnival in the Church calendar. A straw figure named Maslenitsa was patron of the celebrations and was burned at the end of the festival, after much feasting and drinking. In some places during Shrovetide a torch was carried around the village or bonfires were lit, linking the festival to ancient solar cults and pagan celebrations of life in spring.

Easter itself had few links to fertility rites – some scholars suggest this is because Church authorities stamped out pagan rituals on this the Church's most holy festival, when Christ's resurrection is celebrated. Nevertheless, Holy Thursday – the last before Easter – was a time for cleaning, and may have been linked to ancient rites of purification prior to spring work in the fields. On the Tuesday after Easter, moreover, peasants celebrated Radunitsa, a festival in honour of ancestors, although the Church tried to prevent the unseemly public behaviour that usually accompanied the feast. On this day people took food and drink to the cemetery and ate on their ancestors' graves, leaving eggs behind as gifts for their forebears.

Several fertility rites took place during Rusal'naya week, immediately before Trinity Sunday. People adorned their homes with branches and also decorated a birch tree with ribbons and beads. A doll representing one of the *rusalki* – the water spirits who, according to legend, moved from rivers and lakes to trees at this time of year (see page 66) – was honoured during the festival and then ripped apart in the fields.

The spirits of trees and water were worshipped during the festival of Kupala which was linked to the summer solstice. It became associated with the feast of St John the Baptist which was held on 24 June.

An image of Ivan Kupala rises above a bonfire lit at the climax of the summer solstice fertility festival.

The Peasant and the Saints

St Nicholas, who was famed for his kindness, was the inspiration for Santa Claus. In this Russian folktale collected from Yaroslavl province, his clemency contrasts with the punitive anger of Elijah.

There was once a peasant who loved St Nicholas but had no time for the prophet Elijah. He would devoutly light a candle before the icon of Nicholas on the saint's feast days, but when Elijah's festival came around he went about his business as usual, going out into the fields when he should have been observing the holiday.

One day Elijah and Nicholas were walking together and happened to cross the field farmed by the peasant. Nicholas remarked on the tall crops that promised a bumper harvest but Elijah muttered angrily that he had no intention of letting the peasant harvest the grain – he would send hailstorms and lightning blasts to flatten the field.

Nicholas went to the peasant and advised him to sell the crops to the priest at the village church dedicated to Elijah. The peasant did as he was told. Within a week, a hailstorm had devastated the peasant's field.

The next time Elijah and Nicholas were passing the field Elijah boasted that he had taken revenge on the disrespectful peasant but Nicholas pointed out that the blow had fallen not on the peasant but on Elijah's own priest, who had bought the crop while it was standing. Elijah immediately vowed to restore the field to its former glory.

On hearing this, Nicholas visited the peasant again and told him to buy the field back; the priest

Whatever misfortune the angry prophet Elijah visited upon the peasant, St Nicholas ensured the dutiful man had a bountiful harvest.

was only too happy to sell.

Over the next weeks a miracle occurred. Elijah sent sunshine and gentle rains and the field sprouted a new crop of tall rye – as if a golden rug had been flung across it. When Elijah proudly showed his handiwork to Nicholas, only to learn that he had been tricked again, he flew into a fury. He promised that no matter how many sheaves the peasant put on the threshing floor they would not yield a single grain.

Nicholas now told the peasant to thresh one sheaf at a time, and by doing this the man was able to amass a vast store of grain – so much that he had to build new barns. When Elijah saw this he accused Nicholas of helping the peasant and Nicholas confessed. Elijah laughed. He promised to have the last word but would not tell Nicholas what he was going to do. Nicholas flew to the peasant and gave him one last piece of advice.

The very next day Elijah and Nicholas, disguised as poor pilgrims, met the peasant on the road near his field. He was carrying one large and one small candle. When Nicholas asked him where he was going, the man said he planned to light the large candle before an icon of Elijah for he had given him such a wonderful crop, while the small one was for St Nicholas. Elijah was finally pacified and from that day onwards the man honoured both prophets and lived a fine and contented life.

long and difficult labour in childbirth. The saints' power was concentrated in their icons or sacred images, which the peasants sometimes called *bogi* ("gods"). Some of the old gods became directly associated with Christian saints. Perun, who rode the skies in his flaming chariot, was identified with the Biblical prophet Elijah, or Ilya – who according to the Second Book of Kings in the Bible was taken up to Heaven at his death in a chariot of fire.

Elijah, like Perun, also had powers to send life-giving rains. Peasants believed that Elijah transported water across the parched skies in his wonderful car to the saints in Heaven; sometimes he spilled some, and it fell onto the fields below. The saint's day came at the start of the harvest season and like Perun he was honoured as Lord of the Harvest. The day was kept as a holiday in his honour – anyone working in the fields risked incurring his fury. When he was angry he sent, like Perun, storms of hail to flatten the crops. The image of Perun and Elijah also directly influenced the *bylina* of the *bogatyr* Ilya Muromets who rode his horse through the air unleashing a rain of arrows.

Nicholas, revered as "the compassionate" and "the wonderworker", was the peasant's most honoured saint. He derived not from a Biblical figure but from the fourth-century bishop of Myra. Again and again in popular tales of his exploits he proved himself to be approachable, slow to anger and quick to provide practical help – a friend in need for peasants hard-pressed by poverty, illness or other troubles. Nicholas even came to the aid of peasants who had angered other saints (see page 46).

His popularity is reflected in the fact that he had two feast days. One of these, on 6 December, marked the beginning of Yuletide, which was linked to Christmas and Epiphany. He was also patron of horses, cattle and of growing crops and thus had a spring feast day on 9 May. In many areas, this festival fell at a time when horses were pastured overnight in the fields. He also protected fishermen.

Slavic peasants revered the Virgin Mary and another female saint, St Paraskeva, whose cult in Russia appears to have had more to do with ancient veneration of Moist Mother Earth than the life of the Christian saint.

Russian icon of St George and the Dragon, c.17th century. Some scholars have argued that this story, with its echoes of the Aryan god Indra's defeat of the demon serpent Vritra, has ancient pagan roots.

Remnants of Elemental Belief

Slavic peasants had to make peace with the forces of nature. For thousands of years they and their crops were at the mercy of pounding rain and hail, flooding rivers, wind-driven storms and icy winter. The ancient Slavs made the elemental forces into gods, and their descendants, still living at the whim of the elements, continued to hold their unpredictable and devastating power in awe.

An old Russian song tells how a young man offended the Smorodina River and paid the price. When he first came to its banks, he politely asked to be shown the best place to ford and because of his respectfulness the river showed him where to cross. But then the man grew boastful, bragging that he had crossed it easily and that it was nothing but a pitiful stream despite its mighty reputation. Smorodina heard his boasting and when he came to cross back, its waters rose up in a swirling mass and drowned him. As he was dying, the stream spoke, telling him that it was not the river but his own arrogance that had caused his death.

In one tale a peasant was walking to the fields early on a winter morning when he met Wind, Sun and Father Frost. He bowed low in their

Slavic peasants knew that nature demanded respectful treatment. Even if the winters could be unforgiving, the elemental gods of frost and ice were seen as understanding souls who would help those who treated them courteously.

august presence, but he made a special show of homage to Wind. At this, Sun and Father Frost grew angry, and Sun warned the peasant to be sure to honour him – or he would unleash a heat that would burn the peasant up. But Wind retorted that he would save the peasant by sending cooling breezes. When Father Frost chipped in, warning that he had the power to freeze the peasant like a mound of snow, Wind again proved his superiority, reminding his rivals that he could blow warm to melt ice and snow.

Frost personified the power of winter in many tales. In another story a peasant found his buckwheat ravaged by the winter ice and when he told his wife she made him go into the woods to ask Father Frost for recompense. The peasant walked into the forbidding forest until he found an ice cottage standing in the deep snow, decorated with icicles that glittered in the sunshine. When the peasant knocked at the door, Father Frost emerged: an old fellow, white from head to toe. He gave the peasant a cudgel and tablecloth – common instruments of magic in Russian folktales – with which he was able to work wonders.

For the ancient Slavs water was a sacred force, bringing life to crops. The Slavs' ancestors who settled on the Russian plain built their homes along the banks of rivers, travelling and trading along these great waterways. They also knew that when roused to flooding, the streams could be enemies with awesome power. Slavs traditionally made offerings to rivers, seeking to win their favour or avert their fury. Even into the twentieth century, peasants would drop a coin into a river after a safe crossing or successful journey.

Every area had a spring or pool with wondrous healing powers, often associated with St Paraskeva. By a tradition still alive in the nineteenth century, sick people seeking healing would visit the sacred spring, cast a piece of bread into it and ask forgiveness of the water mother or spirit. The ancient midsummer rites of Kupala, which involved ritual bathing and offerings to the water, preserved the cult of water spirits.

Magic waters with restorative, life-giving powers feature in many folktales. All over the world legends tell of a dead heroine or hero brought back to life by magic waters, but Slavic folklore is unusual in that two waters are needed. The first, the "Water of Death", heals the wounds of a corpse – or knits together a body that has been chopped up. The second, the "Water of Life", restores life. Prince Ivan was killed by his jealous brothers who took his golden-maned horse, Firebird and princess (see page 131) but then was saved by the raven and wolf who applied the Water of Life to his dead body.

The waters can have different aspects. Sometimes one liquid fills the drinker with boundless strength while the second brings weakness. There are tales in which one water gives life while the other is literally a water of death, stopping the breath or freezing the lifeblood of whoever drinks it. The wondrous waters are generally guarded by an evil force like a serpent or a warrior maiden. The fearsome Koschei the Deathless often keeps them as does the hideous witch known as Baba Yaga (see page 102).

In one tale a prince travelled far and wide in search of magic waters with the power to restore youth. They were hidden in a flask tucked beneath the pillow of a dread warrior maiden, slumbering under a spell in a castle surrounded by an invisible magical fence. He found the castle, crept into her bedchamber, breathlessly lifted the pillow and took the flask, fleeing on his powerful steed. But because sin weighed him down he could not leap clear over the magical fence: one of his horse's hooves caught on it, breaking the spell and waking the princess. She pursued him in a wild fury but could not catch him. He was

Patriarch Pitrim's drinking glass, made of engraved, gilded and chased silver by Master Grigory in 1672, preserves the ancient belief in the imbibing rituals associated with restorative water.

killed, however, by his own brothers who wanted the waters. They brutally dismembered his body and scattered the pieces far and wide, but then the wondrous Firebird appeared, carrying the waters of death and life in its beak. It collected the many pieces of the prince's body, patched them together with the Water of Death and restored breath to them with the Water of Life.

The Slavs also appreciated the dangerous power of the oceans, personified by the Sea King. In the well-known Russian tale of "Vasilisa the Wise", this mysterious character makes a resolute enemy for a foolish monarch. According to this story, a king was once befriended by an eagle whose life he had spared when out hunting. He

cared for the eagle for three years, letting it eat all the cattle in his kingdom. Then he travelled far and wide with the great bird, and when he finally set sail for home he received a gift from it of two trunks, one red and one green – with instructions not to open them until he had returned.

After many days of sailing, the king landed on a wild and uninhabited island. While he rested he was overcome with curiosity about the trunks that the eagle had given him. He prised open the red one – and to his horror, a vast herd of cattle poured out across the island, so many that he himself was almost pushed into the waves.

Why the Dnieper Flows So Swiftly

The tale of the Dnieper, Volga and Dvina is just one example of many folktales in which the great rivers of the Russian plain are depicted as people, to show how they came into being.

Long, long ago the rivers Volga, Dvina and Dnieper were poor orphaned children. With no one to care for them, they had to labour hard in the fields every day to feed themselves. But fortune was against them and they were often seen wandering in rags, crying with hunger.

Once at the end of a long day Dnieper, who was a boy, sat with his sisters Dvina and Volga on a rough piece of riverbank watching the sun go lazily down in a great wash of red. The three lamented their fate. Hunger gnawed in their bellies and they began to argue over whether they could not find an easier way of life. Seeing the waters flow

gently by, they came up with the idea of transforming themselves into rivers – and decided to travel the world to find a suitable place to change.

For three years they wandered and finally found a swamp that seemed a good starting point for three great rivers. Then they threw themselves down to rest, intending to begin their new lives on the following day. But Volga and Dvina wanted a head start on their brother and as soon as they heard him snoring in his sleep they found a gentle incline and began to flow away.

The next morning when Dnieper awoke, he could see no sign of his sisters. Flying into

a fury he set out after them, running as fast as he could. But then it dawned on him that he would catch them sooner if he were flowing between banks – for no runner alive could outpace a river. Striking the ground with all his might, he became a stream.

His anger was a powerful force, driving him between tall banks and sending him tumbling down steep slopes where rapids formed. His sisters, hearing his pursuit, ran away from each other and into the sea. Dnieper himself suddenly grew calm when he neared the shore and flowed gently into the waters of the Black Sea.

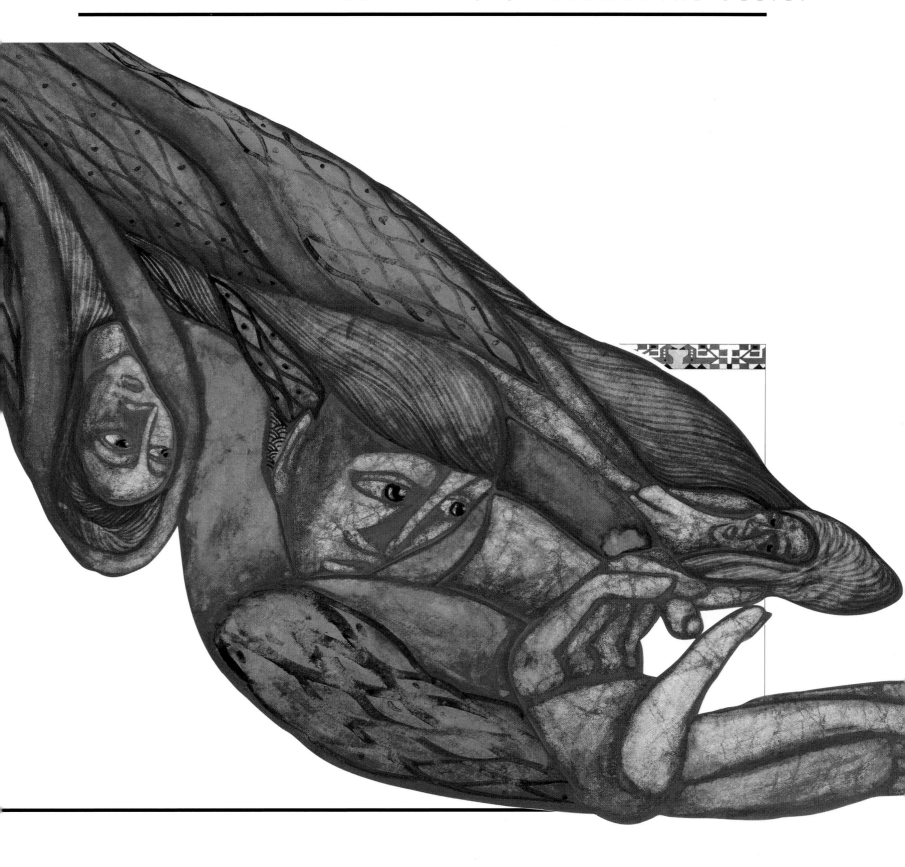

Then he began to weep for he saw that there was no way that he could drive such a vast herd back into his trunk.

The king saw a tall man with a streaming beard emerge from the surf: he was the Sea King, with eyes as cold as the icy depths of the rolling, windswept ocean. On the beach the king explained that he was crying because his cattle had escaped from the red trunk. Then the Sea King offered to help on one condition – the king must hand over the one thing in his own house that he did not know. Now the king thought and thought about this enigmatic offer and, although he could make no sense of it, he agreed to the terms. The monarch of the waves then shepherded all the cattle back into the tiny trunk and helped the desperate ruler to embark once more in his ship.

A typical Russian fairytale ship ploughs its course through the rough seas in a 19th-century drawing. There were many tales that told of the Sea King, but few which painted him as tyrannical as he appears in "Vasilisa the Wise".

When the king at last reached home, he discovered that while he was away his wife had given birth to a son. He wept when he realized that he had been meanly tricked into promising his only child to the cruel Sea King. But he did not dare to tell his wife. Then he opened the trunks. From the red one, the fine cattle poured forth into every corner of his land and from the green one a wonderful garden sprang up. The king laughed and danced about, and in his joy he forgot about the terrible deal he had made with the Sea King.

But many years later, when his son had grown to be a young man, the king was walking by the riverside when the Sea King emerged from the water and confronted him, accusing him of having broken his promise. Now the king told the truth to his wife and his son and they all wept at the cruelty of fate. But they decided that the debt must be honoured, and the son accordingly was taken to the seashore.

Nothing happened at first, and after some time he wandered away, taking a path that led into the forest. There he found a tiny hut on tall legs and discov-

ered the fearsome witch Baba Yaga within. She must have taken a fancy to the handsome young prince for she gave him valuable advice, instructing him to return to the seashore and wait there for twelve spoonbills who would sweep in from the sky and, on landing, be transformed into beautiful maidens. They would slip out of their dresses and dive into the sea; he should take the dress of the oldest one and force her to help him. He would also meet three men named Eater, Drinker and Sharp Frost – and he should take them with him to meet the Sea King.

The young prince did as he was told, stealing the dress of the oldest and most beautiful of the maidens. When the chattering, laughing swimmers clambered out of the water, the eleven youngest took their dresses and, becoming birds again, flew away – but the twelfth tarried, searching for her dress. Then the prince emerged from the bushes at the back of the beach, confessing that he had taken the dress. The maiden smiled and told him she was named Vasilisa the Wise, and her father was the Sea King. Return the dress, she said, and she would help him later. He did so and at once she changed into a spoonbill and flew swiftly away.

Then the prince went on his way and soon, as Baba Yaga had predicted, met three men, who introduced themselves as Eater, Drinker and Sharp Frost. He asked them to come with him and they happily agreed. When they reached the Sea King's court, the cold-eyed monarch welcomed them. But he grumbled that he had grown weary waiting for the young prince and at once set him a seemingly impossible task: to build a huge glittering crystal bridge in a single night – or lose his head.

The poor prince wandered outside the palace

in tears, for he thought that his life was over, bargained away by his short-sighted father. But then Vasilisa the Wise gently approached him. Hearing of her father's demand, she told the prince simply to trust her; go to sleep, she said, and in the morning all would be well. As soon as he fell asleep she summoned masons and builders with a whistle. They worked through the night and by dawn their task was finished – an arch soaring over the palace and scattering the light of the sun far and wide.

The king congratulated the young prince, then set him a new task: to raise a mature garden in one day and night. The prince despaired once more but Vasilisa calmed him again by saying that everything would turn out all right. That night when he was fast asleep she summoned gardeners from far and wide and they planted a miraculous garden.

Now the Sea King offered the young man one of his twelve daughters in marriage – but there was a catch. The twelve maidens, who all looked very alike, would appear in identical dresses on three separate occasions; the prince would have to pick the same daughter each time, or lose his head. He told Vasilisa of the latest trial and she kissed him lightly on the cheek; she was happy to be his bride and would send him a secret signal so that each time he would be sure to choose her. The first time, she would wave a handkerchief, the second, adjust her dress and on the

An embroidered woman's belt from Yugoslavia, *c.*19th century. Elaborate decorations of this type often included charms and talismans to protect the wearer magically from harm.

third occasion a fly would buzz about her head. All went as they planned, the prince chose Vasilisa three times and they were married.

The Sea King was forced to go along with it, but he was not happy. Even at the wedding banquet he tried to cause trouble for his new son-in-law. A vast array of fancy foods was laid out on trestle tables and he told the prince to make sure all of it was eaten – or he would be in trouble. Then the prince asked if one of his friends could join them and, when the Sea King assented, called Eater forward. As a result all was well, for this stout and sturdy gentleman devoured the entire banquet, and even when it was completely gone he could still be seen wandering the hall looking for seconds. Then the Sea King unveiled an enormous store of forty barrels of wines, beers and spirits and told the prince to be sure that not a drop of it was left over. This time the prince brought in Drinker. His remarkable thirst was equal to the demand: he devoured all forty barrels and then asked for more. As a last resort the Sea King called for a bath for the married couple. A cast-iron bath was pulled out and heated over an open fire, so hot that no ordinary man or woman could come close to it. The Sea King looked on happily. But the prince brought forward Sharp Frost. The old fellow approached the bath, breathing out from his icy lungs; soon, glittering icicles hung from the rim and the prince and Vasilisa were able to approach and bathe. Vasilisa and the prince then fled the Sea King's court and settled in the prince's own kingdom, where they lived happily to the end of their earthly lives.

Moist Mother Earth

It was an ancient tradition in Russia and other Slavic countries that the earth was holy and wise – worthy of the greatest respect and to be treated with reverence.

In the remoter parts of nineteenth-century Russia, a man making a solemn vow would swallow a piece of earth – or sometimes place it on his head – as a sign that he meant what he said and would keep his word. Similarly, a newly wed couple would underline their commitment to their marriage vows by swallowing earth.

The ancestors of the first Slavs on the Russian plains almost certainly worshiped the earth in the form of an Earth Mother fertility goddess. Images of oxen found among archaeological remains may have played a part in a cult of the crop-bearing earth. The mother deity may have taken the form of Mokosh, goddess of fertility and women's work, who was adored in autumn, after harvest season, when women settled down to winter tasks such as spinning. She was known to later generations as Moist Mother Earth (*Mat' Syra Zemlya* in Russian).

Many folk customs in the Slavic world attest to the peasants' reverence for the sacred earth. In Volynia and Belorussia, people believed that each year Mother Earth became pregnant and anyone striking her before 25 March would bring terrible trouble on the family, putting at risk the Mother Earth's children – the crops that lay dormant in her belly. In some parts of Russia people performed a harvest-time ritual in Mother Earth's honour every August. In the calm of dawn the peasants went into the fields with a jar of hemp oil. They said prayers to the cardinal directions, each time pouring some of the oil onto the ground. First they bowed towards the east and the rising sun, asking Moist Mother Earth to hold evil spirits in check. Next they faced west and prayed that Mother Earth would use her fierce fires to consume the unclean force of evil. Turning to the south, they asked

Russian ritual towels, such as this 19th-century example, were hung over birch trees or left at crossroads as beneficent offerings to the Mother Goddess, who is shown embroidered with her arms raised. The colour red also symbolizes the goddess, as do the eight-pointed star and birds that accompany her.

Rod and Rozhanitsy

The image of the woman as mother linked two beliefs that were central to Slavic paganism: the cults of the earth and of ancestors.

After the coming of Christianity, Russian peasants continued to make offerings of mead, bread, cottage cheese and porridge to the deity Rod and the twin goddesses the *rozhanitsy*, who appear to have been deities of birth and reproduction. The names are linked to the Russian *rodit* ("to give birth"), *rod* meaning "kin" and *rozhanitsa* "a woman who gives birth". Most writers agree that the twin *rozhanitsy* goddesses were birth spirits, who had power over a newborn child's destiny. Rod seems to have had wider control over reproduction and fertility. The offerings were generally made within the family home, and it is possible that the cult was transformed into belief in the house spirit or *domovoi* (see page 62). Because of their role as household gods, Rod and the *rozhanitsy* have often been linked with a primeval cult of family ancestors.

Mother Earth to soothe the southerly winds and prevent bad weather. As they looked north, they begged her to deliver them from the cold northerlies, bringers of heavy clouds, snowstorms and icy blasts. At the end of the ceremony they smashed the empty oil jar on the ground.

In parts of Russia farmers tried to unlock the secrets of the earth and discover in advance whether harvests would be good in the coming summer. The farmer would dig a hole and put his ear to the ground: when Mother Earth made a sound like a sleigh weighed down with belongings and labouring through the snow, it was a good omen, but when the sound was like that of an empty sleigh flying across the winter landscape, the harvest would be meagre.

Mother Earth had the power to combat evil. It was well known in the Vladimir Province of Russia that a gusting wind on a busy country road was nothing else but the shapeshifting Devil, trawling the land for sinners. The only escape for wary travellers was to confess their sins to the earth. In the same province even in the twentieth century the elderly asked Mother Earth for forgiveness of their sins if they feared death was close. When Russian peasants ploughed a furrow around their village they were trying to unleash Mother Earth's power to conquer illness and unclean spirits. In some regions peasants regularly asked the earth for forgiveness of their sins. Russians believed that if a person spat on the earth they should at once ask pardon of Moist Mother Earth.

The worship of the divine Mother Earth also gave increased impetus to veneration of the Virgin Mary, mother of Jesus, in Orthodox Slavic lands.

The Church festival of the Assumption of the Virgin on 15 August each year was closely associated with the earth and in parts of Russia ploughing was forbidden on that day.

The power of the earth could be transferred to objects found on it. Peasants who came across rocks or stones shaped like a woman's body treated them as sacred objects. People desperate for healing from blindness or paralysis would travel for days to touch the stones and make offerings of animals, crops or money to them. In nineteenth-century Ukraine, archaeologists removed some of these stones from a burial mound of the Scythian era. By doing so, in the view of the local people, they upset the natural balance and brought on a drought.

Icon of the Virgin Mary, from Novgorod, c.16th century. In 12th-century Russia a cult developed around the Virgin with three hands after Bishop John of Damascus had his severed hand restored by praying before an icon of Mary.

The belief in a mother goddess has been central to Slavic spiritual beliefs for millennia. Among the earliest symbols discovered in central Europe are prehistoric female fertility idols which suggest, to some scholars, that before the gods of war took their places at the head of tribal pantheons, the goddess was all powerful – for as the generator and nourisher of the Earth and its people, she was seen to hold sway over life itself. This belief can be traced through Slavic history right up to the present day, when the notion of Mother Russia remains rooted in the national psyche. The pagan Russians saw the goddess in the soil itself (see pages 54–55) and believed it possessed powers of prophecy. In the Christian age, such beliefs were transferred to the figure of St Paraskeva who, for some, eclipsed even the Virgin Mary in spiritual importance. The goddess was the predominant image in nineteenth-century embroidery (see page 54). And her presence survived even in Communist Russia: for she provided the sickle of Soviet imagery, the instrument of the bountiful harvest which nourished industry and fed the people who drove it.

Left: Discoveries of figures like this 30,000-year-old female fertility symbol, from western Russia, have led some scholars to propose that ancient European society was matriarchal. The belief in Mother Earth preserves the idea that all life comes from, and ultimately returns to, a nourishing goddess.

Right: In Christianity, worship of the mother is generally transferred onto the Virgin Mary. Within the Russian Orthodox church, however, it is St Paraskeva who commands the attention of many. The saint, shown in this 15th-century icon, is believed to be a Christian incarnation of the pagan fertility goddess Mokosh, with whom she shares a feast day on 28 October.

Far right: The mother goddess appears in Communist guise gracing a revolutionary poster advertising the magazine *Proletariat Fortnightly,* c.1920. Here she represents the bounty of Russia's harvest which will feed the hammer of industry.

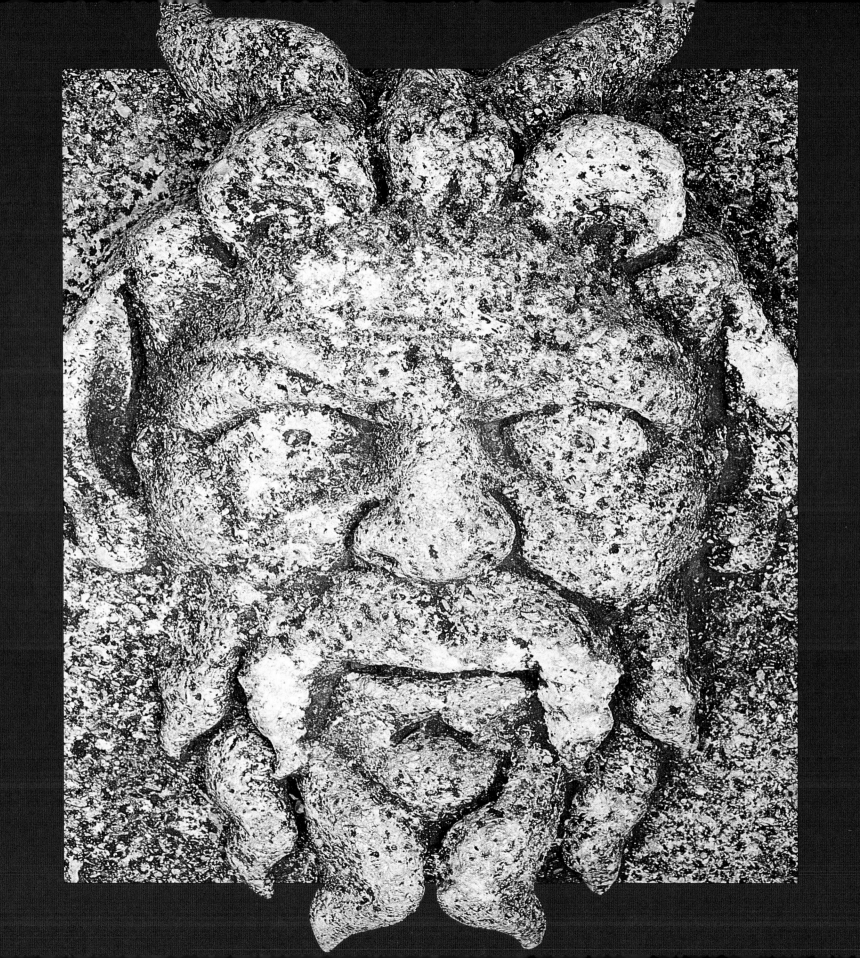

SPIRIT MASTERS
AND LITTLE DEMONS

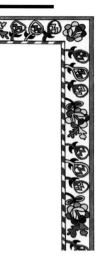

Nestor's eleventh-century *Primary Chronicle* records many early Slavic tribes, all named according to where they lived. Those who settled by a stream called the Polota, he writes, became the Polochane; another tribe was called the Drevlyane "because they lived in the depths of the forest". The environment in which the Slavs lived and worked, however, defined far more than their tribal identity: it shaped a dual sensibility of vivid imagination and firm spiritual belief. Wondrous tales were spawned amid the streams and woods of eastern Europe – within which stalked real and ever-present dangers.

Slavic folklore is populated by spirits of nature whose legends are fuelled by eyewitness accounts and first-hand encounters. These tales of the supernatural, known as *bylichki*, tell of the workings of a whole host of mischievous spirits, each of whom governed a different domain: the *leshii* of the wood; the *domovoi* at home; the *poludnitsa* in the open fields; and the tragic, deadly *rusalka* who swims sadly beneath the surface of pools, waiting to lure vulnerable souls to a watery death. There are spirits for meadow and whirlwind, bathhouse and barn. Some are generally friendly, others quarrelsome or vengeful, but all demand the greatest respect.

More elaborate tales tell of vast kingdoms of the deep or of spirits transmuting into terrible beasts. These stories, *skazki*, conform more closely to a Western understanding of folktales, and they have inspired story-tellers, composers and illustrators beyond the boundaries of the Slavic world. Although fictional, the narratives continue to reflect a very real belief in the arbitrary cruelties of nature.

This supernatural world, however, lay unrecorded for centuries, because the Orthodox church had reasonably firm control of the written word. But as the amount of secular literature increased from the seventeenth century onwards, an oral tradition was discovered. Preserved by peasants for generations, its supposed profanity had an unequalled power to delight.

Opposite: A spirit stares out from a stone wall at Zadar in Croatia. His horns and beard may look jovial and Pan-like to some, but most people today would associate him with the Devil.

Below: One of the principal expressions of Russian folk belief is to be found in domestic woodcarving. This lion comes from a frieze on a house in the Volga region, c.18th century.

59

From Divinity to Demonhood

There are many theories explaining the origins of the spirits who populate the imaginative landscape of the Slavs: some say they are the diminutive descendants of the old Slavic gods; others that they are linked to ancient ancestor or nature worship. But one theory links them to a war in Heaven, lending a dark cruelty to these mischievous enigmas.

This 19th-century rug from Lithuania shows the Devil in his traditional fiery splendour. While the snakes also recall another of his demonic forms, the playing card and drink symbols echo the carousing spirit shared by many figures from Slavic folklore.

The Orthodox Church did not look kindly on the superstitions of the pagan Slavs and turned to their own spiritual imagery to explain them away. The tale of the expulsion of Satan and his demonic hordes from Heaven has since become part of Slavic folklore. Driven out by his Lord and Creator as punishment for his outrageous insubordination, Satan hurtled downwards through the heavens, his damned followers falling at his heels.

The host of acolytes who had assisted him in his rebellion met a variety of different fates. Some fell with him to the underworld, where they labour in the form of *karliki* or dwarves. Some took refuge in the forests where, as *leshie*, they bring about all manner of mischief and misfortune. Others fell into the lakes and rivers of the Earth, where as water-sprites or *vodyanye* they still swim. Many stayed in the sky, becoming *vozdushnye*, winging their way upon the gusting currents of the air, whipping up the whirlwind and directing the destruction of the storm. Still others took up residence in the homes of humanity, as domestic spirits or *domovye*.

The coming of Christianity, while it ultimately offered hope, could not diminish the anxieties of a life lived at the mercy of nature. The new scripture may have had no place for the old gods of water, wind, thunder and fire, but there was still room in the hearts of the ordinary people. A sudden storm could destroy a year's work, a lightning-bolt kill a forest herdsman. The old pagan festivals had fitted in with the rhythms of the rural year; their cruel sacrifices had seemed relevant to the realities of a harsh existence. Christian doctrine explained these natural disasters and family misfortunes as punishment from God for disobedience. The legend of the fallen angels, therefore, offered a simple way of extending the Christian creed to embrace still-important aspects of Slavic life.

There is also a discernible link between the Slavs' ancient ancestor worship and the domestic *domovoi* who is, at times, addressed as "grandfather", and seen as embodying the spirit of the deceased head of the household.

Although the Church insisted these spirits should all be seen as malevolent, their characters are traditionally more complex. At best they are moody and capricious, at worst downright devilish in their conduct. Their goodwill may be secured by assiduous attention, but it can never really be relied on. The offerings that gain favour one day may be spurned the next with unfortunate results: the baby may refuse to sleep, the butter might not churn, the trap fail to spring or the fishing net keep coming up empty.

The most striking features of these spirits, however, is that they influence every aspect of human existence. Not a pot boils in the Slavic household without the interest and interference of the *domovoi*; no cow chews a tussock without the meadow's *lugovik* knowing about it; not a furrow is ploughed without the *polevoi's* prying attention.

The tales told of these demons and demigods fall into three distinct categories. First there are brief eyewitness accounts that describe sudden encounters with particular spirits. A man venturing into an old house sees a mysterious form vanishing into the darkness, for example; a lifelong sceptic has a sudden premonition of his death. Such brief anecdotes serve to confirm the pervasive reality of the spirit realm. Then there are more developed, unabashedly entertaining, stories – while these too might lay claim to truth, they are clearly valued also for their excitement or their humour. Finally there are what Slavic scholars call "legends". Like the story of Satan and his rebel angels, these sophisticated, primarily religious tales may contain much mythological content, but are also heavily overlaid with a Christian message, aiming to discredit forms of belief that the Church dismissed as superstition.

Legends of Light

Slavic creation myths weave together disparate strands of antique paganism and later Christianity into a unique tapestry.

In the myths, God works His creation within a universe organized according to ancient Slavic lore. Instead of willing being to emerge from nothingness, the God of Slavic Christian legend must battle for the rule of light against the powers of darkness. His victory marks the creation of the universe, but even then the conflict is by no means over. When God's favourite creation, the dazzling angel Satan, rebels, his struggle with his master seems evenly matched. And while the outcome of the Slavic and Judaeo-Christian accounts may be the same, their emphasis is different. The powerful pull of paganism can be felt just below the surface of the Slavs' apparent Christian Orthodoxy.

The struggle between the powers of darkness and light has endured in the Slavic imagination, just as it has in many other cultures. Here moonlight strikes the Slovenian coast.

Spirits of the Home and Farmstead

Grumpy and unpredictable yet with the power to influence all aspects of domestic life, the *domovoi* was an awesome presence in the household, to be appeased at whatever cost. With his home behind the stove, he lived at the very heart of every house.

Peasants who had to rise with the dawn to prepare for a day's unremitting toil would go gratefully to their beds as the evening ended, leaving the house to darkness – and the *domovoi*. For in the smallest hours of the morning, while the family and their livestock were all sleeping, this small figure would be up and about, stealing out from his home behind, under or near the stove to wander through his realm, checking that the house was clean, tidy and well managed – and that the right offerings of food and drink had been left for him.

Each *domovoi* had his own preferences, to satisfy his every need. Some required only simple offerings of bread and salt, while others had more exotic tastes – for tobacco or incense. There were other things he favoured too: horses, cats and dogs, all of which would be chosen to match the *domovoi*'s own favourite colour. Animals he took a dislike to, however, found their feed scattered or their tails tied to their stalls. But the *domovoi* had his softer side too: favourite animals, or humans, might wake to find that their manes or hair had been braided in the night.

Known among the Lithuanians as the *kaukas*, and in Poland and Galicia as the *iskrzycki*, the Russians' *domovoi* was held in respect by all the Slavic peoples. He was seldom referred to directly by name, but by such euphemisms as "master", "well-wisher", "he" or "himself". He was most fondly referred to as "grandfather", a title which recalled the origin of the *domovoi* in the Slav's pre-Christian ancestor worship.

The *domovoi* was dwarfish, shaggy and aged in appearance, and generally held to resemble a present or past master of the house. Sometimes, indeed, he was said to wear that person's clothes. But despite this familial link, people took care not to disturb him. An elusive creature who set a high value on his privacy, he would have no hesitation in punishing the over-inquisitive. In one Russian story a young maid, unable to find her buckets

The *domovoi* formed bonds not only with a family but with its pets and livestock too. Favoured animals would flourish under his attentions. This 19th-century embroidered towel is from Russia and shows horses and spirits in colourful harmony.

when she went to look for them one morning, went out to the well where she chanced upon the *domovoi* drawing water. The spirit glared at her in fury, whereupon she ran back in terror to find the whole house going up in flames.

It was unwise to annoy the *domovoi* even in more trivial ways: those whose offerings were deemed in any respect inadequate, whose domestic standards were casual or who managed to offend this irritable spirit were liable to find the timbers of their houses unaccountably creaking, furniture knocking, pots banging, doors slamming, needlework tangled and farmyard equipment turned upside-down. Peasants in the Ukraine's Kharkov Province told the tale of the wealthy merchant who, every Saturday night, according to his family's ancestral practice, left out a bowl of unsalted porridge in the attic for his *domovoi*. Once, however, when he had to leave home in a hurry, he entrusted this task to his cook. Whether bumbling in sheer forgetfulness or acting deliberately out of some grievance with her master, she broke the established rule by putting salt in the porridge. When the merchant returned from his journey he had scarcely crossed the threshold when, from the attic, the pot of cold porridge came crashing down upon his head.

But a tried and trusted *domovoi* was an invaluable ally, guarding a family's well-being and warning of impending disaster. Fortunate families would do all they could to take their spirit keepers with them when they moved. Inviting the *domovoi* to accompany them on their journey, they would carefully rake out the glowing ashes of their stove, pour them into a jar and bring them to the new home where the "grandfather", having been formally welcomed to his new abode, would take his place behind the stove to safeguard the household's continuing prosperity.

The association between the *domovoi* and the stove was both close and highly significant. In a region where winters were long and harsh, the stove formed a natural domestic focus, and as such it constituted a symbolic centre at the heart of the

The Slavs had spirits for all areas of domestic life from the bathhouse to the barn, and propitious relations with these mischievous demons were essential for a harmonious household. A belief in not upsetting the delicate balance of nature permeated Russian arts and crafts and is suggested by this 18th-century birdhouse in the form of a woman.

household, offering in its incandescent interior a warning glimpse of the underworld beyond our own, its glowing embers a reminder of ancestors who had been cremated long before. In parts of Russia, indeed, traditions which lasted well into the nineteenth century forbade the violent poking of logs in the stove: broken-off chunks, it was believed, might fall unchecked through the fire, sending ancestors of the family plummeting downwards to the real inferno beneath. Yet the stove – and the *domovoi* – was only one such focus, for it was understood that the whole house remained the active domain of a recently departed soul for forty days after the person's death, until it left after a proper funeral ritual had been conducted.

The Ungrateful Farmer

Although the domovoi *was considered the most benevolent of the domestic spirits, his behaviour was by no means predictable. To underestimate his hand in a family's fortunes was unwise, but to spurn him altogether was the height of foolishness, as this tale of a farmer who moved house suggests.*

Outside the city of Kupiansk, in the Ukraine's Kharkov Province, lived a proud and prosperous young peasant. Hard-working and self-reliant to the point of stubbornness, he never stopped to consider how others had helped him – the advantages his ancestors had left him with, or even the assistance his *domovoi* had given him around the farm.

Soon the farmer came to feel cramped in the house his family had lived in for generations, and he thought nothing of leaving it for another he had built nearby.

It did not for a moment occur to him that it might be prudent to invite his *domovoi* to join him in his move. His own efforts had brought him this far, he assumed; his own efforts would suffice in the years to come. Without a thought for the past or the future, he pulled down the old house and chopped up its timbers for firewood.

From the first, the move proved a disaster. The crops withered in the field, the livestock sickened in the stalls, the implements broke as soon as they were used – in short, everything that could go wrong, did. The young man's own health started to suffer with the strain of it all, and his fortunes went steadily into decline.

After three years he began to worry, to wonder what might be going wrong. He had his answer one night as he walked past the site of the old homestead. From the heap of ashes which lay where the old stove had once stood, a mournful voice could be heard complaining how the previous occupants had left their old grandfather alone and gone off by themselves. Startled yet strangely moved by this mystical voice, the young man went on his way wondering what it might mean. He became so troubled that he went to the village elders to ask them how his old *domovoi* might be appeased.

On their advice he returned to the ash-pile one night with an offering of bread and salt and begged the *domovoi* to make his new home his own. From that day forth he never looked back. His health recovered, as did the state of his farm. Once more his house flourished, restored by the protection of the *domovoi*.

The farmer's fortunes only changed when he invited his old *domovoi* to join him in his new home.

Opinions differed widely as to whether the *domovoi* was assisted in his duties by a wife or even a whole family. According to some accounts, his wife, the *domikha*, lived under the floor, venturing forth at night to do her spinning in the kitchen. Her infant child might occasionally be heard mewling. Some brave, or perhaps just braggartly, souls claimed that if a rag was tossed over the place from which the cry came, the *domikha*, unable to find her baby, would answer any question asked of her in order to ensure its safe return. Given the power and tetchiness of the *domovoi*, however, such a scheme seems ill-advised.

The Dangers of the Farmyard

But there were demons far more fearsome than the *domovoi*. The *dvorovoi*, the spirit of the farmyard, was a less friendly spirit altogether. Newborn lambs and calves had to be brought indoors away from his predatory eye, while his attentions to mortals seldom turned out for the best. One young woman who had the misfortune to attract the interest of a *dvorovoi* had her hair lovingly plaited by him every night as she slept. But when his human beloved decided she would like to get married, the spirit smothered her in his jealous rage.

More malicious still was the *bannik* of the bathhouse – a place considered, paradoxically, to be unclean, the refuge of witches and the damned spirits of the evil dead. At a more prosaic level the Russian bathhouse did indeed tend, all too literally, to be a hazardous. Its dangers were a result of its somewhat crude heating system which produced the stiflingly steamy and oppressive atmosphere so beloved by the peasants who used it. Fatal fires and deaths by suffocation were by no means unheard-of, and it is hardly surprising that it should have become invested with such powerful superstitious dread.

The *bannik* was held to be not so much mischievous as murderous, sometimes smothering, sometimes scalding those he found bathing alone, in other cases even peeling the living skin from their bodies as they slowly expired in unspeakable

Spirits influenced all aspects of domestic life but not all were as easily appeased as the *domovoi*. The *bannik* was particularly nasty. He lived in the bathhouse which, as this 17th-century picture shows, was popular with the peasants.

agony. The prudent bather was always careful to leave some water behind for the *bannik* – although even this did not ensure good treatment.

The most dangerous of the domestic spirits was the *ovinnik*, the keeper of the barn. He was a large black, cat-like creature who would bark like a dog, his eyes shining like embers – and indeed, fire was the key to his evil. Traditionally, corn was dried out using a furnace inside the barn which meant there was an ever-present danger of the building burning to the ground, bringing inevitable economic disaster and often, of course, human tragedy too. Stories therefore abounded of the *ovinnik*'s mean-spirited savagery: of the woman burned alive in her barn for beating flax on a forbidden holy day; of the peasant who outwitted an *ovinnik* to escape with his life, only to lose his own son to the vengeful spirit several years later.

Siren of the Stream

The *rusalka*'s heartstopping beauty masked an inconsolable sadness. But if personal tragedy was the making of this most enigmatic of water spirits, then vengefulness and spite were her chief motivations and seduction her most powerful and beguiling tool.

In her outward appearance, the *rusalka* matched the natural beauty amid which she lived, her fair tresses flowing in an eddying, endless stream, her fine features framing her fathomless eyes. Simply to see her was to ache with desire. Her victims, however, never did simply see her. They felt in the summons of her sad, yearning eyes an overpowering longing that equalled their own; they found a poetry in her graceful manner that stirred their own deepest feelings; above all, they heard in her haunting song an invitation which could not conceivably be refused. Stretched sensuously on a rock or riverbank, combing out her waving locks with languid, elegant strokes, or weaving flowers into her hair, she was the very picture of eroticism; turning lazily on a mill-wheel or surging effortlessly across a pool, she presented an irresistible image of physical freedom.

The sensuous *rusalka* was a favourite subject of Russian folk art. This 19th-century wood carving is taken from a frieze that once decorated the front of a farmhouse in the Volga region.

Even the wariest traveller, caught out alone by a discreet riverbank or lakeside, might find himself plunging heedlessly, even joyfully, to his doom. For the embrace of the *rusalka* meant inevitable death. Those borne down to her magic boudoir beneath the waves might leave this life in a transport of pleasure but would certainly never return. For while the *rusalka*'s palace was said to be a place of entrancing beauty, its vast marbled chambers hung with crystal chandeliers, its walls and floors set with gold and precious stones, no such splendour was in store for her human victim. And seldom would their family even find the lifeless corpse, floating among the waterside reeds.

Slav lore knew other water nymphs. The Serbian *vila* was more beautiful and more malicious; northern Russia had a squat, hairy hag who used brute force to subdue her victims. But it was the sinister beauty of the *rusalka* of the south which most stirred the wider popular imagination. She even became the tragic subject of later fiction and opera. Literary interest, however, tended to concentrate on her specifically sexual nature.

The *rusalka* of traditional mythology, however, was far more than an aquatic femme fatale. The soul of a stillborn baby or of a child who had died unchristened in early infancy, she might well have a tragic story of her own. In many cases she had lived as a mortal girl until the day she slipped on a wet riverbank and drowned. She then found herself condemned to watch the world from the water, unable ever to return to it.

Every year, in early summer, however, it was said that the *rusalki* would leave their homes in the rivers and streams to dance together in the woods and fields. Darker, more verdant circles in the grass would mark the places where they had cavorted in rings. Garlanded with greenery and fresh blossoms, they celebrated the triumph of summer over the deathly cold of winter.

Rusal'naya Week

While rusalki *danced in the meadows and forest clearings, mortals held festivities of their own, decorating their homes with birch-branches and festooning trees with brightly coloured flowers.*

Although *rusalki* were tragic figures, the festival which celebrated them, Rusal'naya week, was an occasion for tremendous celebration. Dancing happily together, the village girls would bear garlands to rivers and to woods.

There was a more solemn side to all this jollity, though, for this was the time when rites were offered to dispatch the "unclean" dead. Infants who had died before they could be baptized; adults who had committed suicide or been killed as witches or sorcerers: none of these groups could be given full Christian funerals. Nor could those men and women who had been drowned and whose bodies had never been found.

Herself of course an unclean soul in origin, and by her abductions and murders the maker of many more, the *rusalka* had an obvious association with such celebrations, although her role was highly ambivalent. Not only did beauty and evil combine in her, but also fresh early summer and unclean death. So when the *rusalka*'s work of replenishment was done, the villagers were only too glad to banish her for another year. Hence the final ceremony of the week, when she was consigned to the river in effigy.

Festivals such as Rusal'naya week provided opportunities for courtship dances, as depicted in a mosaic by Yegor Vekler, c.1830.

Wonders of the Deep

The *rusalka* was not the only spirit lurking in the waters of streams or ponds. The corpulent *vodyanoi*, for example, was a deadly joker who caroused with drunken laughter; and there were also other sprites who took serpentine form to visit the unwary human world.

While sharing the same streams and rivers as the *rusalki*, the *vodyanye*, the most familiar male water spirits, occupied a very different place in Slavic mythology. With their laughing faces flushed with drink, their paunchy naked bodies and their earthy and uproarious manners, the *vodyanye* were, in both form and disposition, about as unlike the beautiful *rusalki* as could possibly be imagined. Their gatherings were remarkable for their revelry and sport, and so rowdy on occasion that they sent great waves rolling downriver that could carry off bridges and weirs.

The *vodyanoi* was not completely idle, however. He kept cattle in his underwater dwelling, and each night he would drive them ashore to graze in nearby fields. He was also a keen keeper of bees – and indeed the peasant's first swarm of the year was always put in a bag and thrown into the water as an offering to him.

Yet so far as was possible this spirit avoided hard work. He much preferred to laugh and drink, and especially to play practical jokes. One Russian tale related how a fisherman once found a dead

Beneath the calm waters of lakes such as this one at Bled in Slovenia lurked the mischievous *vodyanoi*. He could drag men down beneath the waves by sheer physical force, or create mirages and mists to lure ships and boats to their destruction.

body floating in the water. Lifting it carefully into his boat, he laid it out tenderly to take ashore. Then, all of a sudden, the corpse came to life and, laughing delightedly, leaped back overboard. Despite such tricks, fishermen were looked on by the water spirits as their natural allies. Although the *vodyanoi* was not above tearing their nets through sheer spite, he would usually leave them alone as long as they kept him supplied with gifts of tobacco and proportions of their catch. Millers were also accorded a certain degree of indulgence – although they too had to pay their tribute. Mills were favourite haunts of the water-sprites, who loved to playfully shoot down their rushing mill-races, and turn over and over on their revolving wheels. So close did some millers seem to these spirits that they were thought to be sorcerers and shunned by their mortal neighbours.

The Tsar of the Sea

This famous bylina tells of Sadko, a poor man from Novgorod who owned nothing but a gusli. In his hands this simple instrument produced the most enchanting music.

One day, Sadko sat by Lake Ilmen playing the psaltery-like *gusli*, trying to keep his despair at bay, when he noticed a disturbance across the water. The waves parted in front of his very eyes, and there before him stood Morskoi, the Tsar of the Sea. The monarch thanked Sadko for his playing, and bade him cast a net into the lake. Sadko did as he was told and made a wondrous catch of glistening treasure.

Some years later Sadko, now a wealthy merchant, was voyaging across the Caspian Sea when his ship was suddenly becalmed. The fearful crew drew lots to find out who on board could be the cause of the disaster – and Sadko drew the shortest. The trader then confessed: he had for years neglected the observance he owed to the Tsar of the Sea. When they heard this, the seafarers threw him overboard. Even before he hit the water, a brisk wind filled the ship's sails and off they went once more.

The merchant sank to the seabed where, in a wooden cabin, he found Tsar Morskoi. He had been waiting twelve years to hear Sadko again, he said; and he must play to him now, and enchant his heart once more. Sadko took his *gusli*, and strummed out his sweetest music. Tsar Morskoi smiled in rapture, and danced in delight, causing storms for miles around. The happy water king then offered Sadko the choice of his thirty daughters in marriage. But Tsar Morskoi's wife told him to choose the plainest, Chernavka, and warned him not to kiss her. Sadko did as he was told and the following morning awoke to find himself on the lush banks of the Chernava River, in Novgorod, where he was soon reunited with his own beloved wife.

Tsar Morskoi dances to Sadko's *gusli* playing, by Franck C. Pape, c.1910.

Osip the Watersnake

If the Slavs of the countryside saw glimpses of the spirits of the deep, the feared *rusalki* and *vodyanye*, they also imagined worlds of infinite mystery and terror beneath the waves. For each spirited tale, such as the Tsar of the Sea (see page 69), there were more chilling warnings about the dangers that awaited the unwary bather. One such tale came from Russia's Tula district.

An old woman had a daughter, a carefree girl who loved to play with her friends. One beautiful summer's day the girls went down to the village pond to bathe. Stripping off their clothes, they laid them carefully on the ground and plunged into the refreshing water. They began shouting and splashing about, and were far too busy to notice a long, lithe snake stealing discreetly from the water and curling up in a coil on the daughter's clothes.

Mother and daughter were foolish not to take the water spirit's bargain seriously, for soon afterwards, disguised as snakes, more spirits returned to claim the reluctant bride and carry her back to the pond and their spirit-realm below.

When the girls emerged dripping from the water and began to put their clothes back on, the old woman's daughter suddenly noticed the snake lying on her clothing. She tried to drive it away with a stick, and then with stones, but all to no avail. The young girl was growing increasingly frantic when she received the biggest shock of all: the creature opened its mouth and spoke to her. If she agreed to marry him, said the snake, he would gladly give her clothes back. The young girl was astonished and as her friends laughed derisively she forgot her fear. And deciding that the snake was in no position to hold her to such a preposterous commitment, she agreed. So the snake gave up her clothes and slid back into the water.

When the girl got home she told her mother what had occurred. The old woman laughed scornfully and advised her daughter to forget that the whole thing had ever happened. But a week later an army of hissing snakes appeared, wriggling and weaving their way up the lane to the old woman's cottage. Mother and daughter frantically bolted the door, but the snakes simply rolled into a ball and hurled themselves at the window. They came flying through in a shower of broken glass and, fanning out across the floor, they cornered the weeping daughter on top of the stove. In an instant they pulled her down and carried her off to the village pond, plunging straight down into the murky water. The old woman stood weeping a while, but had no alternative other than to turn and head disconsolately home, cursing her daughter's ill-fortune and her own foolish heedlessness. She mourned her through dismal weeks and months, never feeling the least alleviation, and three years later she was mourning her still.

Deep beneath the surface of the water, meanwhile, her daughter found herself in a different world. Her reptilian abductors had taken the forms of men and women immediately on entering the dark waters of the pond and proceeded to treat her courteously, showing her round the dazzling crystal chambers of their magnificent home. Then they introduced her to her bridegroom. He was a handsome young man and she had no qualms about taking him as her husband. She married him willingly and in three years bore him two children, a boy and a girl.

Although life was pleasant in this world beneath the water, she missed her mother. She pestered her husband for permission to go and see her, and finally he agreed to let her visit her old home ashore. He accompanied her up to the surface of the pond, and there by the bank they bade one another farewell. He told her that on her return, she should call out his name, Osip, and he would come to her side at once. He then dived back into the depths, while she set off for the village with her beloved children.

The old woman was thrilled to see her long-lost daughter – and two such fine grandchildren too. She listened eagerly to her daughter's reports of her new life deep below the pond. She was happy there, her little girl told her, and while of course she had missed her mother, she would not change the life she had now for anything. When her mother asked her husband's name, she said that it was Osip, and that she would summon him by that name when it was time to leave.

The old woman urged her daughter to retire and rest – she must be exhausted, after all, having just journeyed from another world. Once the young woman was asleep her mother quietly took an axe; she sharpened it carefully on a whetstone, then went out of the house and walked down to the pond. She called to her daughter's husband in the words she had been given, and at once the snake was there by the bank, peering out of the still water. She swung the axe and struck his head clean off. Then the old woman went home, well pleased with her night's work: her beloved daughter had been saved from this monster of the deep.

But when the young woman awoke next morning, she found she was already missing her husband and determined to return to her underwater home. The old woman pleaded with her to remain a while longer: there was no way of

This Russian ceramic stove tile is decorated with colourful birds. Unlike snakes, these symbols of freedom were often feted as benevolent spirits. Osip's wife, however, became a cuckoo, forever singing a sad and tragic song alone.

knowing when they would see each other again. Next day, however, her daughter would delay her departure no longer. She took her children down to the pond, and called out as she had been told. When there was no response to her summons, she became worried. She knew that something must be badly wrong. And then, peering out across the water, she saw the severed head of a serpent floating. She sat down on the bank in an agony of bereavement: on land or in water, her life could be nothing to her now. Only the air was left in which to wander: she and her children must henceforth live as birds. Her infant daughter thus became a tiny wren, her son a nightingale and the young woman herself a cuckoo, calling out her grief the length and breadth of the land.

71

Wild Master of the Woods

A devious, dangerous prankster, the *leshii* made his home in the forest depths. Appearing as a vulnerable old man, he would delight in helping out travellers seeking directions but, invariably, his knobbly fingers would point the unwary to a helpless, stranded doom.

Down the generations, many hundreds of lone wayfarers have lost their way in the dense forests of eastern Europe, some never to be seen again. Whenever such a loss was reported, the *leshii* always took the blame. This spirit who dwelt in the deepest parts of the forest appeared in one guise utterly devilish: he was cloven-hooved and sported horns and a thrashing tail. He could also change shape at will, even assuming the likeness of a tree. He could alter his stature too, from the height of a bell-tower to the slightness of a blade of grass. Often he preferred to remain hidden and call out mockingly to some frightened wanderer.

The *leshii* made the forest wholly his own. Protector of its animal and plant life, he made particular favourites of the bear and the wolf, who acted as his special servants. And, much of the time, they protected him as well, for while the *leshii* could look after himself, he did relish raucous drinking sprees. Then, lying drunk and helpless on the forest floor, he was easy prey to some wandering water-sprite or rival woodland spirit.

The world of these nature spirits was never an orderly or harmonious one. Uprooted trees, broken branches and other storm damage were a clear indication that *leshie* had been fighting among themselves. Like *vodyanye*, *leshie* also indulged in wild parties, with lots of raucous singing, drinking and gambling. When hundreds and thousands of squirrels were seen to be moving westwards across the Urals one year, peasants concluded that the *leshie* on the European side had won them from their Siberian kin at cards. If the roaring hurricane was believed to be the sound of *leshie* brawling, whirlwinds were the joyful swirling of their wedding dances.

A Fortunate Escape

Despite the *leshii's* reputation for cruelty, many stories told how humble peasants succeed in outwitting him. When one day an old woman from northern Russia, near Arkhangelsk, got lost while picking berries in the woods, she was relieved when a stranger emerged from beneath the trees and offered to set her right again. But instead he led her to his cottage in a deep forest clearing. He took the old woman inside and presented her to his wife, who was nursing a baby. Here, he told the mother of his child, was the nanny he had promised would assist her.

Many dangers lurked within the vast forests of the European plain and those who had to pass through their depths were careful to appease the spirits with offerings.

The Happy Hostage

One day, a young girl wandered off into the forest and disappeared. Despite their best efforts, family and friends failed to find her and eventually gave her up for dead.

Three years went by before a hunter from the girl's village happened to find himself in the same sector of the woods. There, on a log across the path, he saw an odd-looking spirit. Realizing that this was a *leshii*, the hunter quickly raised his gun and fired. He saw the *leshii* fall, then crawl off into the undergrowth. So the hunter followed.

The trail led to a hut in a clearing and inside the hut he saw the *leshii*, stretched out in death, and beside him a young woman weeping. When the hunter asked her who she was, she looked at him blankly: so he took her to his village where her parents recognized the daughter they had lost long ago. At first she could not understand anything he told her, all memory of her life among humans wiped away. Slowly, however, she recovered. She married the hunter and they lived happily together for many years. As they got older, they would wander in the forest, looking for the hut where she had been confined. Yet though they searched high and low they could not find it: it had vanished as if it had never existed.

When the hunter rescued the young woman, she remembered nothing of her life among humans and felt nothing but grief for the dead *leshii*.

The old woman served them for three years but in time her homesickness became too much to bear. The *leshii's* wife was sympathetic to her sadness, for she was also a mortal who had been kidnapped long ago. She told the old woman to refuse all food and claim she could not eat. As the days went by and the woman started wasting away, her mistress complained to her husband that he had found her a nanny too sick to eat, too weak to work. Feeling henpecked, the *leshii* dragged the old woman back through the forest, dumping her unceremoniously by her own door.

Most tales did not end quite so happily. The prudent traveller would therefore make the sign of the cross and offer prayers for protection before setting foot in a forest. Clothes were turned inside-out and shoes worn on the wrong feet, while horses were unhitched from their carts and their collars and harnesses reversed. Those who lived in the woods made their peace with the spirit by offerings of tobacco or food. Even so, they could never take the *leshii's* goodwill for granted. Woodcutters who offended him by felling a favourite tree, herdsmen whose stock trampled his special places or hunters who killed a beloved pet – all risked harassment, injury or worse.

But a person in trouble could actually summon the *leshii* to their aid by arranging birch branches in a circle, top innermost, like the spokes of a wheel. If they stood at the circle's heart, threw away their cross and called to the spirit, the *leshii* would then appear, ready to do their will. He would prove a powerful ally – but the price he would require would be the person's soul.

73

The Harvester of Souls

While the winter in eastern Europe is noted for its harshness, summer can be just as unforgiving. Under the scorching sun, farmers would break from work at midday to seek shade and protection from the fierce spirit who enforced the daily curfew.

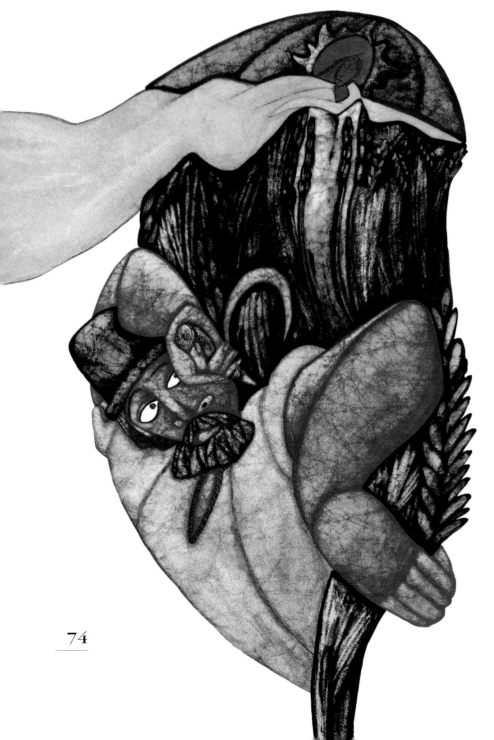

The *poludnitsa* was tall, slim and stately as a stalk of waving corn. Her dazzling white cloak billowed as she strode through the fields in her care. Whereas most spirits loved the secrecy of night, she was most at home at the very zenith of the day. She remained secretive, however: those unfortunate enough to meet her were generally driven mad – if they lived to testify at all.

Those whom she actually found working at the forbidden noonday hour would be subject to her strictest punishment. More horrific in her impassive calm than any raging demon, she would twist the heads from their thrashing bodies, or break their bones one by one.

Her male counterpart, the *polevoi*, seemed almost gentle by comparison. Like the *domovoi*, he could be friendly, yet if seen might signify misfortunes to come. Once a woman who sat by her window late one night saw a *polevoi* flashing by in a troika. A few nights after this warning, which went unheeded, fire swept through her whole village with terrible loss of life.

The *polevoi* was often distrusted as an unclean spirit because he was small, shaggy and invariably dirty. His body matched the colour of the local soil, and grass grew in tussocks from his head instead of hair. This did not make for a pretty sight. Once, a herdsman in Russia's Belozersk district, out looking for his straying cows, suddenly encountered a *polevoi* standing whistling in a field. A long white cloak flapped in the wind which gusted about him. His livestock for the moment forgotten, the poor peasant fled for his life.

Although the farmer was desperate to find his lost herd of cattle, the sight of the *polevoi* made him forget them. He knew that a glimpse of this spirit of the field could mean disaster.

74

A traveller caught amid the open fields as darkness fell might be tempted to lie down beneath the vast, vaulting sky. This was unwise – spirits roamed here just as thickly as they did in the deep woods. The offspring of the *polevoi* loved to play in the fields and were likely to smother anyone they found in a spirit of childish curiosity and fun. Many a mortal sleeper, moreover, was trampled as the spirit galloped thunderously across the plains at night. His horse was the racing wind and he shrieked in his exhilarated delight – the sleeper who survived the onrushing hooves would like as not be driven mad by the terror of his awakening.

Yarilo and Kupala

Christianity had a pervasive influence on Slavic culture, but two pagan festivals endured well into modern times substantially unchanged.

The late eighteenth-century bishop of Voronezh in Russia was not deceived by the superficial gloss of Christianity covering the springtime carnival and midsummer festival his flock celebrated so rumbustiously. Both were heathen abominations, he said – and he was not far wrong.

The feast of spring linked the earth's rebirth with sexual passion, personified in pagan times by the dashing god Yarilo who rode a white charger, wore a floral crown on his head and held a bundle of corn in one of his hands.

The midsummer events celebrated John the Baptist. Yet his identity had become conflated with the story of Ivan Kupala, an ancient Bacchus-like hero who Russians had long celebrated with orgiastic dancing around bonfires on midsummer's eve. Plants, trees and healing herbs were sacred to this figure – a pagan deity who maintained his hold over the people well into the Christian age.

Before baptizing Christ, John the Baptist, shown in this 17th-century icon, spent months in the wilderness. The feast of Ivan Kupala celebrates this affinity with nature.

The Devil Himself

The Devil was all too vivid a figure to the Orthodox Christians of the Slavic lands.
The peasant whose everyday universe already swarmed with spirits, saw Satan as a real
presence and believed his influence to be at work everywhere.

The traditional image of Satan was a powerful one: the eyes glowing like coals, the goatish, cloven hooves, the devilish horns and tail. He was shown in countless icons conducting his minions at the Last Judgement, when the fallen souls of earthly sinners will be offered up to his tormenting flames for eternal damnation.

It was believed, however, that he stalked the Earth in many different guises. Black cats and dogs were among his favourite forms and these creatures were banned from Slavic households whenever thunder threatened, lest the prophet Elijah's avenging lightning-bolts, hurled down at demons, burn up the houses that harboured them.

Other forms the Devil took were those of horses, pigs, snakes, wolves, hares, squirrels, mice, frogs and many more. The cow, most benign of beasts, he always avoided, as he did the cock, loud herald of the cleansing dawn. He also steered clear of the donkey, for it had carried Christ triumphantly through Jerusalem.

Demons crawled up special little crevices to reach the swamps and thickets they infested in the

The village of Arbanassi, in Bulgaria, proved one of the centres of Christian Orthodox art, its paintings noted for the vividness of their images. This depiction of the Last Judgement is from the Monastery Church of the Dormition of the Virgin, c.1832.

world above. In some tales, unfortunate mortals fell down these dismal shafts; in one story, indeed, a peasant pushed his wicked wife down one to her deserved damnation. Once they reached the world above, devils married human witches at noisy, riotous weddings. Held at crossroads, these ceremonies could make the earth shake violently. Large families resulted from such marriages made in Hell, breeding villainy and mischief for humankind. Storms and blizzards lashed the land when the demon children played. Their elders woke the dead with their late-night card-schools.

Spirits of Light and Darkness

But alongside the Orthodox Church's image of Satan as the ultimate in evil, a less judgemental view was also to be found. Early Christian heretical movements, like the Slavic Bogomils, saw creation and life in dualistic terms, as a struggle between opposing forces of darkness and of light, equivalents in power and moral validity.

There was a "bright" spirit and an opposing "dark" one, and it was from their fruitful opposition that the whole universe had flowed. So while all knew and believed the Biblical tale of Satan's black revolt, he at the same time retained some of the qualities associated with darkness in the old beliefs. Many held, therefore, that if God had formed the even ground, Satan had carved out the hills and hollows which gave it character. According to another common tradition, Satan had dived into the primeval sea, and brought back the mud from which God would fashion His creation.

To all intents and purposes, though, the Devil had to be feared as an evil spirit, whatever role he might have played in some remote past. He could steal into a person's body through the tiniest of apertures – small wonder the pious made the sign of the cross when they opened a door or window, or even yawned. He could smuggle himself in through a mouthful of bread or a gulp of water — the utmost vigilance was needed at all times.

More figurative thresholds admitted him too: pregnant women in childbirth, newborn babies

A beatific God watches demons torment a wealthy man whose soul has been lost to the fires of Hell. This coloured woodcut of the story of "The Rich Man and Lazarus", c.1760, indicates the moralistic spin Christianity gave to Slavic belief in demons.

just entering the world and brides on the brink of marriage were among his favoured targets. He might assume the form of a beautiful woman to tempt the chastest of young men, or steal between a widow's sheets in the guise of her late husband. He could spur the most responsible to the most horrendous crimes: vodka was an inestimable weapon to him in his ceaseless battle with virtue; so too were epilepsy and madness, convulsions and fevers of every kind. So formidable were his powers, he could persuade the desperate to destroy themselves. The blame for suicides was laid firmly at the Devil's door. He roamed the world at will, working his evil as he went, the most ubiquitous of spirits, and by far the most foul.

77

MYTHS IN MINIATURE

When Russian scholars began the first studies of their own native art forms, they described three distinct features: the icon, folk art and the *lubok*. This kind of artwork, which had been popular since the seventeenth century, looked not just towards religion or mysticism for inspiration, but to folklore and life itself. *Lubki* images were small, colourful woodcuts which were as likely to depict tavern brawls and jesters as they were to show a religious scene or illustrate a proverb. They were hugely popular with the lower classes, but their irreverent view of life meant they were subject to constant official scrutiny – and in the mid-nineteenth century, tight censorship laws virtually killed them off. But not long after, their elegant simplicity and idiosyncratic designs had caught the eye of Russian avant-garde painters who imitated their styles in their paintings and posters, ensuring *lubki* remained influential into the next century.

Left: Early *lubki*, like *The Blessed and the Damned* from the 1760s, depicted religious scenes and were meant to be as instructive as they were entertaining. Their appeal widened as their subject matter grew more eclectic.

Left: This intriguing print purports to bring *News about the Forest Freak and the Sea Freak Caught in Spain,* and it would have caught the imagination of a people who delighted in tales of strange and wonderful mythic beasts. Beneath the illustrations runs an explanation of how these creatures were captured by Spanish soldiers in 1721.

Above: Scenes from country life were popular *lubok* subjects and included many depictions of hunting. Miniatures like this one, *The Hunter and the Bear,* from 1760, provided illustrations for nursery books which Peter the Great used to instruct his children in the late 17th century.

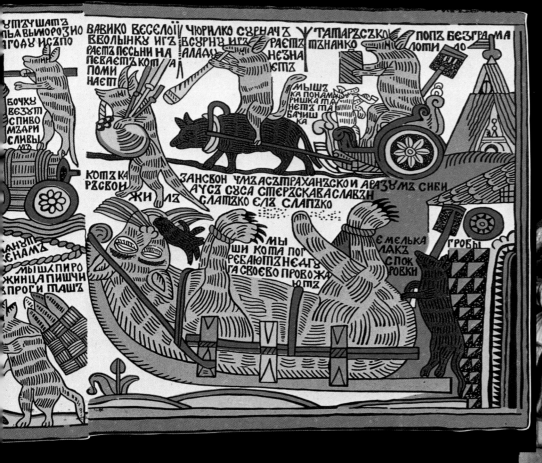

Above: A favourite satirical device among *lubok* artists was to invert familiar animal relationships. *The Mice Bury the Cat* was a recurrent image that here was used to send up the unpopular reforms of Peter the Great.

Right: Russian figurine of a *lubok* seller, *c.*19th century. Some vendors sold their prints from baskets made from lime-wood, or "lub" – which some believe to be the root of the word *lubok.*

KINGDOMS OF THE DEAD

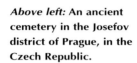

October's gusting breeze tugged at the tree-tops and ruffled the grass; it dulled to a tinpot clanking the sound of the tolling bell, and flapped the sombre black vestments of the bearded priest in the churchyard beneath as he droned out the funeral service he had delivered so many

times before. The grey drabness of the autumn sky; the half-hearted banging of the listless bell; the monotonous murmur of the priest and the blank misery of the mourners gathered around him: all appeared to announce the flat finality of death. As family members moved forward to lower the bumping coffin down into the grave, other relatives moved forward too. Standing at the graveside, they hurled down coins in a tinkling shower – mostly copper, but some silver – money which might be needed in another existence, beyond the grave. And with that, the lamentations began in earnest.

Long before Christianity had come with its promise of eternal life, the Slavic peoples had taken for granted the soul's endurance in another life beyond this one. Death, for them, had been but a doorway to that world, not an end but an embarkation. Whatever the worms might do to the bodily remains, the departed soul set off on another voyage. Christ and His Resurrection, the Last Judgement and Heaven and Hell – the scriptural traditions of official Orthodoxy merely ratified much older assumptions. Although the origins of the ritual had long since been forgotten, this nineteenth-century Russian peasant funeral recalled rites from a much remoter, pre-Christian age. Then it had been believed that the soul sailed to the other world, and that this passage had to be paid, just like any other fare. Important personages might be burned or buried in boats of their own; transport for that voyage to a land beyond the edges of this Earth. Not only the dead but living heroes might make the journey to the otherworld: in the great "wonder tales" of Slavic folk literature, heroes ventured deep into the realm of the dead, enduring ordeals, braving challenges and slaying demons to bring back the most glorious prizes. Yet the journey could be made in both directions: from that world of mystery and darkness, black spirits would spill over into our own, unleashing visions of nightmarish evil and fostering the most unimaginable desires.

Above left: An ancient cemetery in the Josefov district of Prague, in the Czech Republic.

Opposite: The Baba Yaga was one of the strangest figures of the Slavic "wonder tales". From her forest lair, this mythic character guarded the gates between this world and the next. By Ivan Bilibin, *c.*1901.

A Marriage of Life and Death

Slavic belief in an afterlife blurred the distinctions between life and death. The departed, therefore, was celebrated almost as much as the newlywed. Rituals and calendar feasts ensured that the living stayed in close communion with the dead throughout the year.

The Wedding Procession by Wincenty Wodzinowski, c.1895. With the harvest gathered in and fieldwork at a minimum, autumn was a time for weddings, the ceremonies of which shared the same robust sense of celebration as Slavic funerals.

After months of toil amid the unforgiving fields, the harvest was at last gathered in. As the first heavy clouds of autumn came rolling in across the plain and the earth began to harden in expectation of the winter freezes, villagers throughout the Slavic lands would now have time and, hopefully, food to spare – and thoughts could turn to the elaborate ceremonies of love.

But it was not merely practicality which dictated that Slavs celebrated weddings in autumn and winter when their workload was lightest, for they believed that even in the dying of the year, the spirit could be renewed. Furthermore, Slavic beliefs in life and death meant that weddings shared many characteristics with funerals, not least an air of robust celebration. For death, it seemed,

was not a dark shadow to be feared – one Russian Yuletide ritual involved staging a mock funeral, sometimes even with a real corpse, around which people gathered in a pretence of mourning and laughter. The logic was clear: amid life's energy and abundance, the dead were not forgotten. Although long departed on their journey to the world beyond our own, they endured as presences in their descendants' midst: hence the existence of a wealth of ceremony aimed at maintaining propitious links between the living and the dead.

Although Yuletide commemorated the depths of winter, a key feast was also held earlier in the season to mark autumn and the first frosts of winter. St Dimitri's Day, in October, celebrated the great warrior-saint who, in 1380, delivered Russia from Tartar Khan Mamai's invading armies. His holy day, however, expressed gratitude for many other gifts as well, including the successful completion of the harvest and the lives of late relatives and friends. On "Dimitri's Saturday", peasants all across Russia would flock faithfully to church, where their priests would lead them in the solemn commemoration of the dead. The service over, they would pour out into the churchyards in milling throngs to offer their own more extravagant thanks, weeping copiously over the graves, recalling their occupants in anecdotes scabrous and sentimental, laughing and singing raucously and blessing the memory of the departed in increasingly rowdy toasts.

A Spring Saint's Day

Such rituals were maintained throughout the year. The spring Radunitsa was one important Russian festival of the dead which is thought to have dated back to the most distant days of prehistory. Ancient as it was in its origins, however, it was still being celebrated in the late nineteenth century in some areas, much to the outrage of the clergy who objected to the all too obviously pagan mood of ribaldry and licence it fostered. It was frowned on particularly because it involved the women and girls of the community, encouraging them to throw off all their customary feminine restraint. Each year at this time, the female inhabitants of the village would come together and proceed to the local cemetery, bearing food and drink. There they would visit the graves of their friends and relations, mourning their loss in extravagant lamentations, weeping and howling in expression of grief. Then, all of a sudden, as if at some hidden signal, the mood

of the gathering would change completely, deep sadness giving way to high merriment as the assembled women commenced a riotous picnic upon the churchyard tombs. Laughing, singing, dancing and playing games, they offered joyful, and frequently scurrilous, thanks for the lives of the dead. More than this, however, they shared their own living cheer with their ancestors, who were themselves held to be eating, drinking and rejoicing with their living descendants, full participants in the festivities. When the party was over, the scraps of food would be cast on the graveyard ground and the dregs of drink emptied ceremoniously on the tombs. These were offered both to the dead who would partake of the feast themselves and finish off what food was left, and to those spirits who might decide to disturb their slumbering souls in the course of the coming year.

The rituals of Radunitsa thus cemented the bonds between this world and the next, making clear the continuities between the two and honouring the enduring kinship between the living and the dead. While the souls of past generations persisted in the present, watching over their descendants' fortunes and doing their best to protect them from danger and want, those still living did what they could in their turn to preserve the peace of their ancestors' rest.

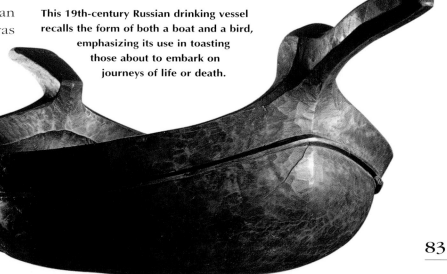

This 19th-century Russian drinking vessel recalls the form of both a boat and a bird, emphasizing its use in toasting those about to embark on journeys of life or death.

The Soul's Dark Journey

A long and often arduous journey awaited the departing soul – it might encounter all kinds of obstacles in its passage and assume all manner of different forms. It was important, therefore, for the dead to be properly equipped at their funeral for the ordeal ahead.

The idea of death as a journey was common to all the Indo-European peoples, although in Slavic mythology it took several different forms. The image of an ocean-crossing was ancient and persuasive, yet so too was the thought of tramping to the next life along a dusty and gruelling road. The dead were sometimes buried in boots so as to be properly equipped for this long march – a custom which endured as late as the nineteenth century among peasants in the remote Czech mountains.

At times, death's highway was identified with the multi-coloured sweep of the rainbow across the sky; at others it was traced in the infinite path of the Milky Way. Four mighty mowers blocked

Slavs believed that when the body died, the soul began a long journey to Heaven. The path had many forms: some said it was marked by the Milky Way or rugged stormclouds; others saw its course stretched out across a bright and brilliant rainbow.

this starry arch, according to the people of Russia's Tula Province, scything down those who sought to make their way across to safety. Elsewhere the road was envisaged as a rugged route over the billowing backs of the clouds, within which malevolent storm spirits (or, in later myths, marauding Tartars) had been imprisoned. Vast black dogs guarded the road in some versions of the story, barring the way to all but the most intrepid.

Yet another view saw the passage to paradise as the ascent of a steep-sided mountain, its faces sheer and unyielding, made of polished iron or even glass. Nail clippings taken from the deceased were commonly included with the entombed corpse which, it was thought, would need sharp talons to make such a precipitous climb. In pagan Lithuania, the bodies of wild beasts were burned with the human dead, so that the souls of the deceased might have the advantage of the animal's claws when the time came to make this sheer ascent. Well into the modern era, Russian peasants wore rings and amulets containing owl claws or their own nail-parings.

But whatever the nature of the journey to salvation, whether undertaken by land or by sea, the soul had first to escape the narrow confines of the grave. With this in mind, peasants often buried their dead with wooden ladders or knotted leather ropes to assist in the climb. Long after the reason for the tradition had dropped out of the popular memory, corpses in Russia were interred with little ladders shaped in dough and then baked into bread.

The Land of Rakhmane

Some Slavs thought the soul came to rest on a land far beyond their own shores.

Along with the paradise of the setting sun, Rai, many Slavic peoples believed that there was also an eastern land of ease. The Galicians, for instance, talked of the land of Rakhmane, far away to the east where the sun rose to begin its daily course. There, it was said, lived a happy, holy people, so saintly that they fasted all year except for one great feast day.

The arrival of this festival, the Rakhmanian Easter Sunday, was signalled by the appearance of a consecrated Easter egg, which floated across the sea from the lands of mortal mankind. Slavic story-tellers associated this unimaginably exotic eastern nation with the Brahmins of Indian legend. Some said that these holy men arrived there thousands of years ago and theirs is the name which over time became corrupted to the Galician "Rakhmane".

These Czech painted eggs show how one ancient Slavic belief remains very much alive. The feast of Rakhmane would begin when an egg reached the shores of the magical island.

According to certain other traditions, however, the soul has no need to escape the tomb, never having entered it in the first place. Some Slavic opinion saw the soul as leaving the body at the moment of death. It would then hover near at hand to supervise the ceremonies by which the body it had once inhabited was consigned to the earth. Only then would it set off on its long journey in the company of an angelic guide.

The Bulgarians believed that the departed took the form of a butterfly or bird before flying away on its long pilgrimage to the afterlife. Beautiful, fragile and fleeting, the butterfly was popular throughout the Slavic lands as an image of the human soul. Other ancient accounts saw it instead as a spark, struck from the mortal body by Perun, the thunder god. Still others saw the stars as so many mortal souls: whenever a new one appeared in the sky a baby was born; each time a meteor fell to Earth, a man or woman died. For the people of southern Siberia, the soul had its dwelling-place in the windpipe. It could thus be seen leaving the body in the last breath of the dying man or woman. Shadows and reflected images were also seen as symbols of the soul, being mysterious in their power to possess all of the body's form without any of its actual substance. Mirrors, therefore, were widely regarded as reflecting the viewer's inner self and the more traditional members of the community distrusted them as accursed inventions of the Devil.

The end of the soul's long journey was a land variously known as Rai, Nava or Peklo, the destination for both the just and unjust. Over centuries, however, the influence of Christian custom separated the names into different realms, along Judaeo-Christian lines. Rai thus became associated with Orthodox views of Heaven, while Peklo took on many of the characteristics of Hell as a place of terror and torment for the damned.

Lands of Destiny

The view of the otherworld as the refuge of the soul, reached after a long journey, is reflected in one of the richest veins of Slavic mythology, and has produced many tales of heroes conquering distant spirit lands.

Skazki were tales of fantasy, stories in which the imagination built huge cities beyond the horizon of our own mundane experience. If the buildings of peasants were of humble wood, then the palaces of fairytale shone brilliantly with gold and silver, coloured rich with jewels and guarded by strange and fearsome beasts.

Such tales would often feature an unlikely hero who felt drawn to embark for a distant land just as the soul would travel beyond death. He or she would travel through places where animals spoke, beasts prowled and where treachery lurked behind every smiling face. And once the far-off land was reached, the hero had to secure his safe return. One such story told of Prince Ivan who, driven by a desire to fulfil his destiny, travelled to the otherworld to rescue his mother who had been carried off by a malevolent spirit.

Prince Ivan climbed the steep cliff-face to the otherworld with the aid of talons that grew fantastically on his fingers. But when he faced the writhing snakes that guarded the three palaces, he subdued them not with magic but with water.

Three Kingdoms: Copper, Silver, Gold

A king once married a beautiful queen who bore him three fine sons, Piotr, Vasily and Ivan. They all lived happily together until, one day, the queen went for a walk in the palace garden and was snatched away by a mighty whirlwind.

The years went by, and when the older princes attained manhood, the sad king bade them set out in search of their mother. But as soon as they left, their younger brother begged to embark on his own quest. The king pleaded with him to stay but he could not dissuade the young boy, and he at last gave him permission to go. So Prince Ivan saddled his horse and set out into the world.

In time he entered a deep, dark forest where he came upon a castle in a clearing. There he found an old man, who welcomed him courteously and listened to his story. He felt pity for Ivan, so gave him a ball and told him to throw it before him, for it would lead him to his mother. Prince Ivan cast the ball in front of him, and it rolled on ahead of him just as his guide had promised.

Ivan had not gone far before he met his brothers, Piotr and Vasily. He told them of the old man's guidance, and they agreed to accompany him on his journey. In time the ball took them to the base of a huge mountain range. Ivan saw before him a cave and as he strode in, he started in amazement as sharp claws of iron clipped themselves to his hands and feet. Then, telling his brothers to wait for him, he began to climb.

It took him a whole month before he finally reached the top. There he saw a rocky ridge stretching away to the farthest horizon, which he followed until, finally, he came to a gleaming castle of copper. A seething mass of serpents writhed before its gate. They hissed angrily but Ivan, seeing a well with a copper bucket, drew up some water and gave it to the snakes to drink. Pacified, they lay down, and he walked on into the castle. The queen of the copper kingdom came to greet him, and he told her of his quest. She did not know where his mother was, but she wanted to help him for she too was a prisoner of the whirlwind. She gave him a copper ball to guide him, and begged him to set her free when he returned.

The copper ball led him on over mountains and through valleys until he came to another castle, built of solid silver and once more guarded by serpents. When Ivan had calmed them with water from the castle's well, he found the silver queen, another prisoner of the whirlwind. She too offered her help and, giving Ivan a silver ball to lead him on, asked to be rescued when he came back. This ball led Ivan to a third castle, this time cast in gold. Again, terrible snakes watched over its gate, but once more Ivan was able to calm them with ease. Queen Elena was kept captive within, a woman more beautiful than the prince could ever have imagined. She gave him a golden ball, but she begged him not to forget her plight.

Ivan followed the golden ball until he found himself before a castle of dazzling diamonds. Serpents with six heads stood guard at its gate, but they lay down once the prince had slaked their thirst. He entered the castle and there, on a throne, sat his mother. She wept for joy at the sight of him but warned him that he was in terrible danger. He would have to defeat the whirlwind in battle if they were to make good their escape.

She took him down to the cellar where there were two tubs of water. The one on the right, she explained, was the Water of Strength. Ivan drank his fill, then his mother told him to switch the vats. The queen then hid her son beneath her robe to await her abductor's return.

The castle shook as the whirlwind landed, immediately taking the form of a handsome man. But as he moved to kiss his captive bride he smelled the blood of a mortal intruder. Ivan jumped forward to grapple with his foe, who at once assumed his rightful form. The whirlwind dragged him desperately the length and breadth of the world before tiredness began to overtake him. Returning to the castle in the hope of replenishing his strength the whirlwind-man headed straight for

The magnificent silver and gold palaces of folktale were often a sumptuous reality for the feudal lords of Europe. These 18th-century gates at the Catherine Palace in St Petersburg were cast in iron and decorated entirely with gold-leaf.

87

the cellar and drank deep at the right-hand barrel, while Ivan took his fill of the other. Within moments he felt the whirlwind weaken, while he himself sensed power surging through his body. He turned and killed the monster, burning its corpse and casting the ashes to the winds.

With his mother at his side, Ivan began to retrace his steps. He released the gold, silver and copper queens on his way and soon arrived at the top of the iron mountain. There he let down a linen cloth and the queens climbed to safety. Piotr and Vasily were waiting at the bottom as promised, but when they saw the beautiful women, they were tempted by ambition and greed. Before Ivan himself could make his perilous descent, his brothers snatched the linen rope from his grasp and hastily made off, leaving their brother stranded high above the clouds.

Ivan roamed the kingdoms of copper, silver and gold alone until, one day, he found a reed pipe by a window in the diamond castle. Sadly, he determined to play on it to alleviate his solitude. But when he sounded it a lame and one-eyed servingman appeared. The strange figure explained that he had once served the whirlwind, but his true master was the pipe, and he was at the service of whoever blew on it.

To defeat the whirlwind, Prince Ivan had to wait until it had run its course and returned home to recover its strength. Hiding in the tyrant's cellar, he then summoned up all his might to dispatch him and rescue his mother.

Ivan asked to be returned to his kingdom, and no sooner had he spoken than he found himself there, in the city's bustling market. But he was alone, without money or possessions, so he asked a shoemaker he happened upon to take him on as his apprentice. The cobbler agreed and, ushering him into his workshop nearby, asked him to make a pair of shoes.

Ivan summoned his servant with a blast on his pipe and within moments he had conjured up slippers fit for a queen. Next morning the cobbler, coming to see how his assistant was faring, gasped in astonishment at the work he had done. He took the shoes to the market, where they caught the eye of a royal servant buying clothes and provisions for a threefold wedding which was about to be held. Prince Piotr was to marry golden Elena, the servant explained; Vasily would wed the silver queen, while the copper queen was to be given away to a general.

Elena recognized in the shoes the magic workmanship of her own kingdom, so she had the

The Isle of Buyan and the Alatyr Stone

Far away at the ocean's edge lay the magic isle of Buyan where, according to the Slavs, all the elements of the earth originated.

Storms waited on the island before sweeping the skies at the weather god's signal; the spring tides marshalled there, waiting to be unleashed on a hapless world. But here were mustered all the gods' more positive powers: the capacity to inspire strength and courage, to protect against wounds and disease. If tempest and flood had their home on Buyan, so too did prosperity and luck in love.

But the isle's most powerful force was centred upon the Alatyr stone, a glowing mass of amber from beneath which water could be seen to flow. It was held to be the source of all rivers, and also a fount of healing – while later Christian traditions associated it with the trickling of blood from Christ's wounds. All Heaven's force, for good and for evil, thus originated in Buyan, source of all that was sacred – as well as much that was to be feared.

shoemaker summoned to her presence and asked him to make her more. If he failed in his task, she said, he would go to the gallows.

The cobbler went away in despair. How on earth could he produce another pair of shoes when he had not even made the first? That night he drank heavily and went early to bed. But when he awoke the next morning he found before him another pair of shoes as miraculous as the first. When he expressed astonishment, his apprentice explained that they had made them the previous night and that he could only not recall it because he had then got drunk. The cobbler proudly took them off to the palace, only to return in still greater consternation: Queen Elena was so delighted she had

commissioned a wedding dress! Once again he drowned his despair in drink while his apprentice and his magic servant worked their wonders. This time the queen was so delighted with the result, she asked the cobbler to build her a golden palace. Even this challenge proved well within the capabilities of Ivan's supernatural assistant, and by morning a golden palace stood on a site outside the town! When a messenger from the city came to ask the cobbler to whom the palace belonged he was so bemused he simply, at Ivan's request, handed over a note which the young prince had given him. It was addressed to the king, and told him all that had occurred.

And so the story ended happily, with Ivan's father and mother reunited. He himself was joyfully married to the golden queen, Elena. The king was dissuaded from executing his two other sons for their treachery, and instead Prince Piotr married the queen of the silver kingdom and Prince Vasily the copper queen.

This tale is typical of many skazki in that the hero is confounded by human nature as well as the supernatural. The different elements of this skazka, however, are resolved through magic. The hero fulfils his mission and finds the tools he needs to overcome adversity in the otherworld.

One of the striking aspects of this story is the clemency shown to the treacherous brothers. While the good in this case certainly end happily, so too do the bad. The tale focuses more on entertainment than moral instruction. As another skazka, "The Magic Box", shows, however, those who sought to profit by misdeeds were, in return, invariably punished and denied the potentially rich rewards of magic.

Music was as important a part of folk ritual as story-telling, giving ordinary instruments such as this 19th-century Polish reed-pipe a magical quality. In the story of the three kingdoms, it is the spirit of such a pipe that rescues Ivan from despair.

The Magic Box

A young peasant apprenticed to a master craftsman quickly surpassed his teacher in his work. Jealous, the older man, who was also a magician, resolved to send his apprentice on a hazardous quest. He was to go down to the underground kingdom and bring back a little box he would find sitting on the ruler's throne. The two went to the ravine which led to the underworld and the youth reluctantly climbed down on a long rope.

He was met by a great crowd who acclaimed him as Prince Ivan, their protector and lord, and led him to the throne room where he found the box. He made his way back to the rope and, having decided to take his new retinue with him, sent them on ahead. His master hauled half the servants up to the surface before a workman came running to tell him his workshop was on fire. The craftsman then ran off, instructing the workman to keep on hauling – but to leave the apprentice behind.

The young man was left marooned underground, but as he tossed the box from one hand to the other twelve men suddenly appeared at his side, awaiting his orders. He asked them to take him back to the upper world, and they quickly complied. The apprentice thought it better not to return to his treacherous master who, learning of his escape, sent men to catch and kill him. But the boy had wandered off into the wilderness. There in a deserted spot he shook the box and ordered that a splendid new kingdom be built – and in a flash, there it was.

Ivan ruled this magic realm both wisely and well. He married a beautiful princess, and lived in such splendour that soon he could scarcely recall that he had ever been a mere apprentice. But one day the son of a poor old woman Prince Ivan had often helped, poisoned his mother's mind against her protector and persuaded her to steal his magic box. Availing himself of its powers, the traitor had his monarch dethroned, stripped and beaten, setting himself up as king in his place.

He was then cruelly cast into a pit where animal carcasses were thrown. Prince Ivan despaired, and began to wonder what was to become of him. But when a giant bird flew down to scavenge among the scraps and snatched up a whole carcass, the peasant prince had an idea, and tied himself to another rotting beast. The great bird swooped again, plucked out this second carcass and flew up into a tree. Shot by a huntsman, it then dropped its festering booty – and Prince Ivan – to the ground. As he walked sadly back towards his lost kingdom he felt something in his pocket. It was the key to the magic box, and it responded when thrown in the air. The servants summoned were delighted to be once more serving their true master: they immediately punished his usurper and restored Ivan to his kingdom, which he ruled just as wisely as he had before.

The elaborate designs on this 18th-century carved ivory box from Russia are a typical feature of Slavic craftsmanship. Boxes and chests themselves perhaps reflect a fascination with the keeping of secrets that arouse great curiosity and wonder.

The Fox Physician

A macabre variation on the Jack and the Beanstalk theme evokes the image of the Heaven tree, which in old Slavic myth connected Earth and sky and was the key to the Creation.

An old man once planted a cabbage-head in his cellar and was astonished at the speed with which it grew. He had to cut a hole first in the floor of his cottage, and then the ceiling, as the amazing stalk thrust itself towards the sky. Soon it was lost among the clouds. Curious to see where it led, the old man scrambled up it until he found himself in a strange land.

There he found a handmill which gave itself a turn before his eyes: out came a pie, a cake and a delicious pot of porridge. The old man ate and drank until he was sated, before stretching out to sleep off his meal. He then slid back down the tall cabbage-stalk to tell his wife what he had found.

Amazed at the story, the old woman insisted upon seeing for herself. As she was too weak to climb the whole way, however, they decided that she should slip into a sack which the old man would grip tightly in his teeth. This would leave both his hands free for the arduous climb.

So long was the ascent that the old woman soon grew impatient. She called out from the sack to her husband, demanding to know whether they still had much further to go. Grunting through his teeth he told her that they were still only halfway to the top. As they neared the clouds the old woman called out again to ask whether they were nearly there. Her husband tried to answer, but as he did so, the sack slipped from between his teeth. It hurtled to the ground and when the old man climbed fearfully down after it he found his wife lying dead. Mourning her impatience, he knelt down beside her body and wept.

Just then a fox came by and asked him what the trouble was. On hearing what had happened the beast promised to use its special healing powers to bring the woman back to life. All the husband needed to do, it said, was to place his wife in the bathhouse and stoke up the fire until it was nice and hot; then he must wait outside while the fox performed its merciful work.

The old man did as he had been instructed, waiting patiently for several hours. At last the fox came out and told him he could open the bathhouse door and take a look at his spouse. As he did so the fox suddenly raced off, laughing wickedly. To his horror the husband saw why: for all that was left of his beloved wife was a pile of well-gnawed bones.

Tormentor of the Night

While Slavic wonder tales told of heroes returning triumphantly from the otherworld, stories abounded of more sinister emanations from the spiritual plane. For the fictional *skazki* reflected a real belief in vengeful spirits who plagued the world with nightmare.

With the working day dictated by the rising of the sun, nightfall signalled the time for sleep. But in the darkness of a winter night many went fearfully to bed – for sleep and dreams were the playground for the *kikimora*'s demonic games.

Although it is thought her name derived from the French *cauchemar*, or nightmare, the *kikimora* remained quintessentially Slavic. Like the *domovoi* (see page 62), she was known for her little pranks about the house: for tangling up knitting or needlework, or plucking feathers from hens in the yard outside. But such practical jokes only served to conceal her true malice.

The soul of a girl who had died before being baptized, the *kikimora* wandered the world bringing Hell's anguish to those who still lived. In Serbia, Montenegro and some other parts of central and eastern Europe, she was thought to issue from a witch's lips in the guise of a fluttering butterfly. Beautiful, diaphanous and yet dangerous and vindictive, she would settle on the face of

Twilight descends over the Kamniske Mountains and Slovenia's Sava valley, waking malicious spirits like the *kikimora*. In the Balkans this restless soul was closely associated with the vampire, although her attacks seldom proved fatal.

City of Lost Souls

Vengeful spirits could plague whole cities as well as individuals – and, as one tale of the city of Slavensk shows, they could also drive people to make desperate sacrifices.

Long ago, the city of Slavensk was founded by slaves from the Danube valley. Legend has it, however, that it was built without the ritual offerings that were the spirits' due. In a few short years the unfortunate city was devastated by plague. Confronted with the ruin of their homes and livelihood, surviving city fathers decided to establish the colony anew, this time taking care to offer the prayers and sacrifices that would ensure a future of good fortune.

One morning they sent out messengers in every direction, charged with bringing back the first living creature they encountered – for this would be the sacrifice to propitiate the spirits. After a short while, one of the envoys returned clutching a young child. The elders would not allow pity to sway their judgement, resolved as they were to omit no part of the established rites. The child was thus buried alive beneath the foundation stone of the new city,

Some say the legend of the founding of Novgorod, shown in this 16th-century etching, has its basis in historical fact.

which was renamed Dyetinets. But the ill-luck which had attended the city's first incarnation persisted until Dyetinets was at last ravaged by fire. Its terrified inhabitants knew better than to stay there and fled the accursed site to found a new city, Novgorod, nearby, which, finally freed from misfortune, flourished for many generations.

some peaceful sleeper to oppress their breathing deep in the night. While these attacks, unlike those of the vampire, were seldom fatal, they were much feared, and elaborate precautions were often taken to avoid them. These included filling the keyhole of the bedroom door with wax, pointing shoes away from the bed or cursing the spirit.

In some Serbian traditions, the *kikimora* could take the form of a horse or a strand of hair. One man found his nights so persecuted that he mounted his own steed and fled. Roaming far and wide through the land, he found no rest at all, the *kikimora* following wherever he went. One night, however, the master of the house in which he was staying heard his sleeping guest moaning, groaning and desperately gasping for air. Stealing into his room to see what might be amiss, he found a long tuft of hair across the man's mouth, blocking his breathing. Taking a pair of scissors, he cut the strand neatly in two and the sleeper immediately started to breathe more easily. Next morning, however, when the traveller went to saddle up his horse, he found the beast lying dead in its stall. At first he was shocked by his loss, but he came to see things differently through the nights that followed: for with his horse, it seemed, the afflicter of his dreams had also departed and he could, at last, sleep in peace.

Feasts of Flesh and Blood

Of all the restless spirits who stalked the dark shadows between the worlds of life and death, none could be more terrifying than the vampire, a dead soul whose sustenance was warm blood or even living flesh. For the Slavs, however, this figure could take many forms.

A peasant was driving his cart past a lonely graveyard one summer's night when he was hailed by a stranger who asked him for a lift. The peasant was a kindly soul, and glad, too, of the chance of company, so he bade the stranger climb up beside him, and make himself comfortable. In appearance the man was unexceptional, his scarlet shirt the only thing that seemed at all out of the ordinary, but he was easy and amiable in his manner and the peasant quickly relaxed. They drove on together into the village, the stranger making cryptic remarks about the gateways of all the houses they passed.

Now it was that the innocent peasant began to notice something odd about the way his new companion was behaving. "Closed", he would say of each house, whether their gates seemed to be fastened or not. Some of the doors they went by swung wide open in the scudding breeze, yet the stranger appeared to consider them shut. Only slowly did it dawn on his terrified driver that what all had in common was the protection of a cross. They neared the end of the village street, and just one house remained; the peasant could see from a distance that its gates were firmly locked and barred. But his passenger tensed with excitement – he had sensed that there was no cross there; and, sure enough, the gates

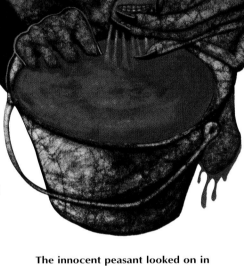

The innocent peasant looked on in amazement as his travelling companion savagely attacked two men, drained their blood into a pail – and began to drink it thirstily down.

opened of their own accord as they approached. Inside two men lay sleeping, one young and one old. The peasant watched in amazement as his mysterious new companion approached the poor youth. Taking a pail in one hand, he struck the boy savagely on the back with the other: he caught the flowing blood in his bucket and drank. Then, turning to the old man, he did the same thing again before turning to go, his thirst finally slaked. He ordered the peasant to drive him home, and he was, of course, too frightened to object. Arriving at the graveside he stood helpless in fear as the stranger made to take him in his arms. He would surely have spirited him away down into the earth with him had it not been for the intervention of day. For at that moment the cock crowed and the corpse released him with a shudder, slithering noiselessly into the coffin whence it had come. The peasant returned to the village, still in shock, to find that the old man and the youth had both died mysteriously in the night.

The vampire is perhaps the most distinctive of all Slavic spirits, and undoubtedly the best known in the outside world. The shadowy figure arising from its coffin at midnight to suck blood from the bodies of those who sleep is a familiar image and one that has its roots in distant mythology.

While some stories tell of vampires taking sexual possession of their victims, they were clearly cannibalistic in their broader intent. They could only be defended against by sacred symbols like the Cross. They shunned the light, and fled at daybreak back to the sanctuary of the grave, but the moment night fell they would return to the world above. An aspen stake driven through the heart with a single blow would put an end to their activity forever – but any second blow would revive them and kill their would-be dispatcher instead. Movement in the grave was a sure sign of a vampire's presence for they would often turn over to lie face downwards, away from Heaven's unsightly glare.

Views of the vampire's origins varied widely through the different Slavic cultures, but they were generally acknowledged to be "undead" beings. Such souls had departed one world without succeeding in entering the other; they had left life without being accepted by death. They were generally held to be suicides who had despaired of God's judgement or drunks who had died in spiritual oblivion: these souls could not be saved or damned in the usual way. Instead they existed in an ambiguous state, hovering halfway between life and death. Some traditions numbered foul murderers among the undead; others included lesser criminals and prostitutes. Witches and sorcerers were obvious candidates too, the evil of this second life a logical continuation of the first. But even the most blameless could be condemned to this existence if not buried with all the appropriate rites. Banished from the air, the undead dwelt in the grave, yet the earth too refused to take

them to its own. Vampires therefore did not decay in the ground – the pristine perfection they maintained in the grave was a mark not of sanctity but of sin.

Theories of how they fed differed: since they had no living bodies, some said, they had no need for normal food. But as they required something to sustain them, they drank the blood of living people. In Russia, however, it was commonly held that vampires were, in fact, ravenous flesh-eating creatures.

There have been many theories produced to explain such beliefs. Some nineteenth-century folklorists argued that the vampire myth was suggested by the weather, by the earth's absorption of moisture from the clouds. Others have argued that the milking of cows offered the original analogy, and that a once positive image was gainsaid by Christianity. The Church does indeed appear to have taken a role in the evolution of the vampire myth, identifying heretics with the bloodsucking undead. It has also left one enduring mark: the insistence that the stake driven through a vampire's heart be made of aspen, the tree it was thought Judas Iscariot had hanged himself from.

Despite the fame of the vampire, this figure was not particularly prominent in Russian folklore. It was better known, and feared, among the people of Belorussia and the Ukraine, and widespread among the Croats, the Kashubs of Poland and, of

The most powerful defence against vampires was the Cross, a symbol which aimed to shine spiritual light on the darkness of paganism. This silver-gilt 17th-century example is specifically Russian in form.

95

The Dead Mother

The vampire of many Slavic folktales is a very different figure from the Dracula of popular fiction. Rather than a damned and vengeful spectre of fear, the undead could be a tragic ghost lost through fate rather than misdeed. And as the following story shows, the fiend is not always male.

A young married couple lived happily together, the envy of all for the love they had for each other and the harmony in which they dwelt. Before long, the woman bore a child – a fine, healthy boy. But within hours of the birth, his mother had died. Her husband grieved sorely for her loss, and agonized over what should become of the baby. While he could offer the child his love, the boy needed a mother's milk and tenderness and these he could not give.

An old woman was found to take charge of the boy, but he would take no food from her. He showed no appetite for milk, but simply cried and cried. Yet somehow as the weeks and months passed he seemed to be thriving, and for a short time each night his complaints would somehow cease.

One night the boy's father determined to find out what was happening and he resolved to keep a vigil to see what he could learn. That evening, he lay down as if to sleep, with a candle by his bed, its flame concealed in an earthen pot.

For some hours all that could be heard was the incessant sound of the baby's crying, but at midnight the door creaked and a dim figure crept in. It made its way across the floor to the cradle where the baby lay complaining; it raised the child up and he lay silent and still.

The father uncovered the flame to reveal the strangest sight imaginable: there sat the dead mother, calmly suckling her living son. She looked up sadly as she saw the candle for she could not endure its light. She walked wordlessly from the room without so much as a backwards glance; then the father rushed to the cradle and found the baby dead.

The light that let the father see his son's midnight visitor also forced the shadowy figure to flee. And as the woman did so, she left the infant dead in its cradle.

A ruler of Wallachia in what is now Romania, Vlad Tepes is often cited as the source of the Dracula legend. But far from dying under a wooden stake, he inflicted that fate on others, going down in history as Vlad the Impaler.

course, the non-Slavic peoples of Transylvania whose beliefs were fuelled by the tales told of the notorious Vlad Tepes, the original Count Dracula whose very appearance struck fear into people's souls. In many Slavic folktales, however, the vampire does not always appear an overtly sinister character and, as one story shows, he can assume the most surprising guises.

Marusia's Lover

The most beautiful girl in the village, Marusia could have her pick of the neighbourhood's young men. But none had ever attracted her as much as the young stranger she met one year at the first night of the St Andrew's week celebrations. Tall,

handsome and courteous, he caused a flurry of excitement among all the girls present. His preference for Marusia was clear, however. All evening they danced and chatted together, and before the night was out he had asked her to be his wife. Marusia, who had also fallen in love with him, was glad to accept but said she would have to tell her parents, who would want to know all about him.

He told her he was a merchant's clerk from a neighbouring village, and Marusia duly passed on this information. Intrigued, her mother urged her to find out more; giving her a ball of thread which she said would help her in the task. When she bade her fiance farewell next time, her mother said, she should loop one end around a button on his clothes so she could follow it to his home.

Marusia did as her mother suggested and the trick worked well. When the thread had unrolled she began to follow its path. Down the lane and across fields and ditches it took her – then passed straight under the bolted door of the church. Marusia climbed up to a convenient window to discover what was going on inside – and nearly fell down in fright. Before the altar in an open coffin a body had been laid out for a funeral the next day. There knelt her lover, calmly eating the corpse. Marusia meant to steal secretly away, but in her panic she slipped and fell noisily to the ground. Plunging headlong across the fields, she arrived home safely, still fearful that she might have been seen.

All that day she stayed indoors, terrified; but when evening came, she decided to venture out to join her friends at a St Andrew's feast in the village. To her horror the handsome fiend was there again, the party's beaming, unflagging life and soul. When he asked her to step outside with him at the end of the evening, she wanted to refuse, but her friends pressed her so hard she was left with no option. He asked her straight out if she had been at the church the previous night, and although she denied it he evidently did not believe her. He fixed her with a cold stare and declared that her father would die the next day. Then he vanished into the dark night.

Marusia awoke the following morning to find her father dead, as predicted. He was placed in a coffin to await burial. Horrified by this terrible turn of events, she went out to find her friends, hoping to leave behind for a moment her fear and grief. But her cursed suitor was still with them, all smiles and sympathy; no one could have imagined that he felt anything for her but tenderness and love.

When at the end of the evening, he asked her once more to leave with him, she tried to refuse, but her friends gave her no peace until she complied. Outside, he pressed her again to admit that she had seen him in the church, but she continued to deny the fact. Furious, he told her that this time her mother would die, then stormed off, leaving her alone to fear the worst.

Dawn broke the next morning to reveal fresh horrors – her mother was indeed dead. Again Marusia fled the scene of the tragedy to find her friends but once more the fiend was with them, all insincere sympathy and hollow charm. As if in a nightmare the events of the previous day repeated themselves, and once more she found herself at last alone with her tormentor. When she persisted in her show of ignorance, he told her to prepare for the worst. By the next night, he said, she too would be dead – and with that he strode off, leaving her shaking with terror.

Never had Marusia felt more alone. The one person she could think of to turn to for help was her grandmother. On hearing her story, the old lady advised her to go to the village priest and make him promise that, if she did indeed die, he should give orders for a hole to be dug under the door of her house, so that her coffin and those of her parents could be removed without crossing the threshold. After that, the three bodies should be buried at a crossroads.

The priest readily agreed to these requests, and Marusia went home to prepare for death. She had a third coffin brought to the house and laid down in it voluntarily. That evening she passed away, as the stranger had foretold. The priest kept his word, and buried Marusia and her parents at a place where two roads met.

In time a strange flower bloomed on the unfortunate girl's grave. One day a nobleman's son noticed it in passing, and was struck by its beauty. He plucked it from the ground and took it home with him. Lovingly tended, it flourished in the young man's care.

One night after struggling vainly to sleep, the young man's servant got up and went walking through the house. To his astonishment, he found that he was not the only one awake at that hour. He saw the flower stir and sway in its pot, its rustling petals become the folds of an elegant gown and its heart the face of a beautiful maiden. The servant watched silently as this ravishing creature wandered calmly through his master's house, then returned to her pot, a flower once more.

The next night the servant's master watched with him but as they looked on the young man could not contain his feelings. He ran up to this wondrous maiden and seized her by the hand. He begged her to marry him, and Marusia agreed. She made one condition, however: he must swear not to ask her to go to church for four years.

The two lived happily together for some time and Marusia bore her husband a fine baby son. But then the foolish young man began to heed the village gossip about his wife's failure to go to church. The next Sunday he insisted on her going, accepting neither refusal nor excuse. With sinking heart she obeyed him and went to the church, to see the vampire sitting on the very windowsill from which she had watched him eat his fill. He reminded her of their acquaintance so long before and asked her again if she had watched him in the church that night. And when she insisted she had not, the enraged vampire told her that her husband and son would both die the next day.

Marusia ran straight off to see her grandmother for advice. The old woman gave her two small vials, one containing Holy Water and the other the Water of Life. When Marusia's husband and baby son died the next day, the vampire appeared before Marusia and asked her if she had been at the church that fateful night. This time she admitted that she had been but as she did so she sprinkled him with the Holy Water and he at once crumbled into dust. She then sprinkled her husband and son from the other vial and they came back to life – and with the vampire at last banished for good, they all lived long and happily together.

The flower that had been picked from the unmarked grave at the crossroads stood in the house a long time before its secret was discovered by a servant. Thanks to her grandmother's advice, Marusia survived the vampire's vengeance.

99

The Strange Face of Immortality

One character peculiar to Slavic folklore was the enigmatic figure of Koschei the Deathless. Although a spirit of fiction, rather than one genuinely believed to stalk the countryside, Koschei offered intriguing insights into the Slavic view of death – for he was a man who lived separately from his life.

Koschei was undoubtedly one of the oddest characters in Slavic myth, for his own life was said to exist apart from him, hidden in a distant land. If Koschei himself was to be vanquished, the stories claimed, this spirit double had first to be found and killed – no easy feat, since it lay within an egg that was itself concealed inside an animal trapped within another, rather in the spirit of Russian Matreshka dolls. One of the best-known tales told how Prince Ivan clashed with this fearsome adversary in his search for the lovely Princess Vasilisa.

Ivan and Vasilisa

It was ordained from Prince Ivan's earliest childhood that he should one day marry Vasilisa, the daughter of King Kirbiet, and when he was fifteen he resolved to seek out his bride. He journeyed to a town in whose main street he found a man being flogged. An onlooker explained that he had failed to repay a debt. Anyone could save him by paying off the arrears, but in doing so would forfeit his own wife to Koschei the Deathless. Prince Ivan could not stand idly by, however, and, since the sum involved was an insignificant one, he decided to pay. The debtor, who was called Bulat, promised in return to serve the prince with all his strength for he had magical powers that could help him win his bride.

The two rode off together and soon found Vasilisa in the impregnable castle where her father kept her. Its defences were no match for Bulat's resourceful wits, and soon they were galloping off into the distance, Vasilisa laughing and smiling at Ivan's side. But as they pitched camp that night, Koschei, remembering the debt he was owed,

crept up and snatched Vasilisa away as Ivan and Bulat slept soundly under the stars.

When Prince Ivan woke to find her gone, he was distraught, but Bulat told him to be calm for he knew exactly where she would be. They rode for many days and nights until they found Koschei's castle. Stealing inside disguised as simple shepherds, they made their way to the kitchen. There Bulat threw a ring Vasilisa had given Ivan into a cup destined for the lady of the house. When her maid brought her drink, Vasilisa recognized the ring. She called the men to her and heard what Bulat had to say. They would kill Koschei and free her, Bulat promised, but they would need her help. Her husband kept his life separately from his body, so could not be destroyed in the ordinary way. She had to find out where it was hidden. Vasilisa promised to help, then told them to hide. Her husband had been hunting, but was expected home at any moment.

When Koschei returned, she made much of him, showering him with tenderness and love. She had worried so much about him, she said, fearing he might be killed in the wood by wild beasts. He mocked her fears, telling her that he was completely invulnerable, since his life was not kept within his body. Then where was it? she asked him. The explanation he gave her was quite astonishing: on an island in the sea stood an oak tree, he said, and buried beneath the oak tree was a wooden box. Within the wooden box was a hare, he went on, and within the hare a duck was to be found. Inside the duck was an egg, and there, inside the egg, he concluded, lay his life. Prince Ivan and Bulat set off at once to find it, and after many adventures they succeeded. They brought

the egg back to Koschei's castle, and struck him hard on the forehead with it, killing him. But as Prince Ivan made off with Vasilisa, Bulat dreamed of the cunning vengeance being planned by Koschei's twelve wicked brothers.

When they got home, Prince Ivan wanted to show his friend his most prized possessions, but as soon as he led in his dog, his childhood playmate, Bulat drew his sword and cut off the animal's head. When Bulat went on to kill his beloved horse and then his favorite cow, Ivan despaired of his once trusted friend: whatever service he might have done him, Bulat had to die. So he gave orders for his immediate execution. Before his death, however, Bulat told the prince about his dreams, and of how his animals would have been used to kill him. He then turned himself into stone. Ivan now understood the actions of his friend, and mourned him deeply.

Watercolour by Ivan Bilibin of Koschei the Deathless charging into battle, from the illustrated tale, "Maria Morevna", c.1901. In this story, Koschei also kidnaps the object of Ivan's desires and, once again, is eventually slain by the conquering hero.

The years went by, Ivan and Vasilisa raised a family together, but their grief for Bulat did not lessen. Then one day, many years later, the statue suddenly spoke. If Ivan and Princess Vasilisa were to kill their children and smear its surface with their blood, it said, their friend would at once be restored to life. Grief-stricken as they were, they decided to do as the statue said. They killed their children and daubed the dead stone with their blood. Bulat came to life with a smile of gratitude and love, and thanked them for their loyalty and trust. He took them to the next room where they found their children playing. And they all lived happily together ever after.

101

The Bones of Baba Yaga

An incongruous mix of the domestic and the deathly, Baba Yaga was perhaps the strangest spirit of them all. A hideous old woman who ensnared the unwary deep within the forest, she was often outwitted and could even, without knowing it, be a force for good.

This early 18th-century Russian woodcut uses the Baba Yaga to satirize Catherine the Great who is shown attacking a squirrel-like crocodile, representing Peter the Great. Baba Yaga here rides a pig, although she usually travelled in a mortar. There were no crocodiles in Slavic lands which accounts for the shape of the beast representing Peter.

The young brother and sister had been wandering blindly in the woods for hours when, suddenly, the undergrowth began to thin. Ahead, they could see a clearing with a little house at its centre. Exhausted as they were, they broke into a joyous run. Only when they reached the very edge of the trees did the girl pull up with a start and stretch out her hand sharply to hold her brother back. She nodded at the house before them, and he followed her gaze with mounting shock and disbelief.

An ordinary looking cottage it was, to be sure – but it stood on spindly legs like a hen's. The fence which ringed the tiny garden around it seemed to be built from bleached human bones. The pair froze in terror, but as they sought to summon up the courage to turn in their tracks and run, a strange noise robbed them of what strength they had left. As the distant drone rose into a roar, a sudden wind lashed the tree-tops; the earth seemed to tremble beneath their feet. The children gripped one another, then the boy pointed upwards in horror: hurtling through the air towards them came what seemed to be a flying kitchen bowl, ringed with flames. As it came closer they saw it was a sturdy grinding mortar, paddled along by a hideous old hag with a giant pestle. Tall

Baba Yaga and the Brave Youth

Baba Yaga does not always triumph over her adversaries. Indeed, in some stories she is outwitted by the simplest cunning, as the tale of the youth who lived with a cat and a sparrow illustrates.

One day the cat and the bird went off into the forest to cut wood, warning the youth that should Baba Yaga appear he must say nothing at all. Baba Yaga duly arrived, went straight to the kitchen and rummaged through the drawers. The youth watched in silence until he saw her taking one of his spoons. But as he cried out in anger, Baba Yaga saw him and bore him away in her fiery mortar. He called out to the cat and sparrow to save him and after much pecking and biting, they managed to set him free.

Next day they went off to the woods again, leaving the youth with the same warning, but once more he proved too impetuous to take heed. He cried out at the hag as she counted out the spoons. Again she abducted him, and he had to be rescued once more.

When this happened on the third day, however, he was not so lucky. As Baba Yaga bore him off through the air, he called on his friends in vain – for they had ventured far out of earshot.

The monstrous old woman took him to her house where she handed him to her eldest daughter, instructing that he be roasted while she went out on an errand. Asked to lie down in the roasting pan, the brave youth

affected incomprehension. How was he to arrange himself? he asked. Exasperated by his stupidity, Baba Yaga's eldest daughter got in herself to show him: and he promptly pushed her into the oven and slammed the door. She was duly roasted to a crisp. The young man subsequently played the same trick on the witch's second daughter, again with

fatal results. And when the youngest daughter met the same fate, her mother saw that she would have to do the job herself. But she too fell for the youth's simple deception, and was roasted in the oven as well.

The cat flew at Baba Yaga with her claws and the sparrow pecked furiously with his beak, and thus they succeeded in setting their friend free.

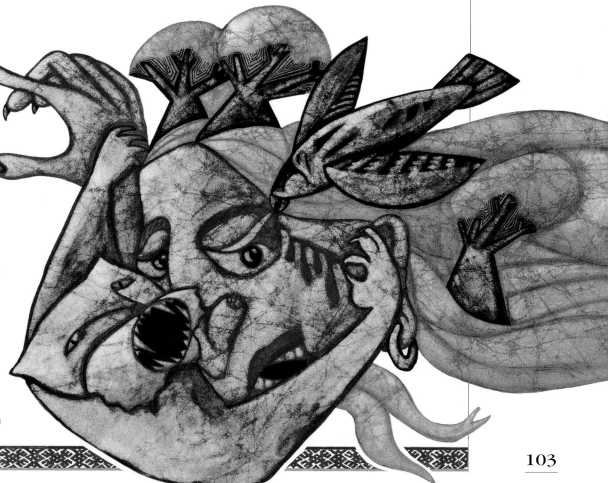

and gaunt was her figure, her grimacing face a mass of writhing wrinkles; a long proboscis, apparently of iron, hooked over a cavernous mouth lined with the longest, sharpest fangs. Her wild white hair streamed in the air behind her as she drove her strange conveyance along, periodically turning to cover her tracks with brisk sweeps of a fiery broom. In an explosion of cackling laughter, she touched down beside her long-legged cabin: it turned and stooped to receive her as if welcoming her home. As she crossed the threshold she glanced back over her shoulder with a malicious smile: could she have known where the two children were hiding all along?

In one form or another, Baba Yaga was known throughout all the Slavic lands. In the Ukraine she was a fiery flying serpent; in Serbia old "Iron Tooth", as she was known, was an angry storm. In all her guises, however, she left behind her the sickly smell of death wherever she went.

Baba Yaga is usually imagined living in her house on chicken's legs set deep within the forest. She was so influential, however, that her presence was also perceived amid cornfields where her passing would cause uncut wheat to sway.

Some scholars believe that her associations with death had their origins in the initiation ceremonies by which youths passed into manhood in pre-Christian times. These rituals, which acted out the process of death and rebirth, were carried out in remote cabins at some distance from villages. Baba Yaga's house, with its fowl's legs and grisly garden fence, certainly suggests an entrance to another world beyond our own. In addition, her hideous appearance has been linked to a once-powerful goddess of the underworld. In some stories she has power over day and night, which also hints at divine origins; so does the fact that in various myths she seems almost benign, helping to overcome obstacles in her path.

The hint of a broader influence within Slavic culture is strengthened by her associations with natural forces beyond the forest. When the wind bowed down the cornstalks, for instance, people said that Baba Yaga was chasing after children: when she caught them, they added, she would crush them in her mortar and cook them to feed her insatiable hunger for human flesh. Cornfields were a favourite haunt of Baba Yaga, so much so that the last sheaf of the harvest was often offered to her, woven into the shape of a female figure and then dressed up in rags to provide the effigy of an aged crone. Although this connection linked her to the *polevoi* (see page 74), it was not with the fruitfulness of the fields that Baba Yaga was associated but with the grim harvest of death; the stalks which fell in swathes before the reaper's swishing scythe were like men and women mown down by fate.

In some traditions she had daughters who shared her deathly appetites while in others there were three Baba Yagas – a trio of hideous and hungry sisters who the hero had to outwit. One such tale concerns a young man's love for the daughter of a tsar.

The Maiden Tsar

A handsome young merchant's son once fell in love with a beautiful tsar's daughter who came to visit him from over the sea. But the boy's wicked stepmother did her best to confound their love. When the Maiden Tsar next came to visit, the stepmother put a spell on him, ensuring that he slept deeply. His lover was unable to rouse him, and returned home in despair. But, when she learned of his stepmother's intervention, she sent the young man a message. If he still wanted her, he could have her, she told him, but he would first have to journey to her land. She would be waiting for him, far away across the sea in the otherworld.

He set off at once. His journey took him through a deep wood. There in a clearing stood a hut on chicken's legs. The old woman within was a fearsome sight, but he greeted her nonetheless and asked her if she knew the way to the otherworld. She did not, she told him – but her younger sister might be able to help. She pointed out a secret way through the forest, and soon he came upon a second house. Like the first, it teetered on chicken's legs; and within there was a hideous hag. She could not help him either, but directed him to a third sister who lived still deeper in the forest. Moved by his youth, she also gave him a warning: this younger sibling had cannibalistic tastes and might seek to eat him. So she gave him a horn to blow in case of danger. He thanked her for her kindness, and continued through the forest. In time he came to the third sister's hut. This Baba Yaga caught the youth and made to kill and cook him, but he remembered her sister's warning and sounded his

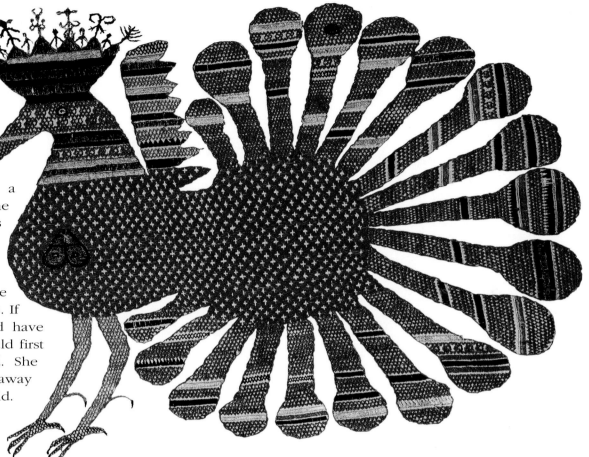

An early 19th-century embroidered towel in the form of the Firebird. Such a bird came to the merchant's son just as he was about to be cooked by the Baba Yaga for dinner.

horn. An immense flock of birds appeared, the lovely Firebird in the midst of them all. It bade the young man climb on its back, then rose swiftly up into the sky. The hellish crone bellowed in her rage, but the bird bore him safely away. Flying far across the sea it came down in another clearing, where an altogether more benign old woman gave the boy food and drink and a night's rest. The Maiden Tsar no longer loved him, if he wanted to win her he must find out where her love was hidden and restore it to life again. By good fortune her daughter worked for the Maiden Tsar and she was able to find out her mistress's secret: her love lay hidden in an egg, within a duck which lay

105

inside a hare. The hare in turn, she said, was concealed in a coffer which was buried beneath an oak tree. If the young man could only locate this tree, therefore, he might recover his lost love.

The boy followed this advice, and went off to look for the egg; when he at last found it he brought it back to the old woman, who invited the Maiden Tsar to dine with her. She served her the egg, and the young woman's passion for the merchant's son was kindled anew. The old woman then ushered him in to the room and the two lovers fell into each other's arms, resolved never again to be parted.

Vasilisa the Beautiful

The best-loved tales of Baba Yaga were those in which she was cheated of her prey. In the tale of "Vasilisa the Beautiful", she even helped a maiden achieve the justice she deserved.

Vasilisa's great beauty was bitter gall to her stepmother and stepsisters: they abused and humiliated her in every way they could. Confining her to the kitchen, they did their best to starve her and worked her like a slave. But to their horror, whatever they did she seemed to blossom, growing daily more charming and more fair. Her secret was the little doll her late mother had left her, which was feeding her, doing her chores and keeping her from all harm. And so when her stepmother sent her into the forest on one errand after another, Vasilisa always returned safe and sound. The wicked woman secretly hoped that Baba Yaga would seize and eat her, but the doll kept her well out of harm's way. Then one night, the stepmother and her daughters snuffed out every candle in the house, and told Vasilisa to go and ask Baba Yaga for a light. Quaking with fear, she went into the dark forest as ordered. When she arrived at the crone's house she knocked at the door. Of course she could have a light, said the old woman, but

The fiery gaze of the skull that Baba Yaga gave Vasilisa guided her home through the forest, then burned up her mother and sisters when she got there. Watercolour by Ivan Bilibin, c.1901.

first she must come and work for her. She must tidy, cook and clean and do everything right, or she would eat her up. Vasilisa was too afraid to do much work, but fortunately her doll was with her and did not let her down. The hungry old woman was furious and doubled the girl's workload for the next day. Once again, however, Vasilisa's doll took it all in its stride: when Baba Yaga saw all the work had been completed, she was reduced to shaking her head in frustration and disbelief. She tried to break her servant girl's strength once and for all on the day that followed, but was finally forced to concede defeat. Asking how Vasilisa had managed, she was appalled to hear of the doll left her by her loving mother: no such purity could be allowed in her ghastly abode of death. Pushing Vasilisa unceremoniously out of the door, she handed her a skull with coal-eyes gleaming. Here, she said sourly, was the light her stepmother and stepsisters had sought.

Vasilisa returned home and handed over the skull as she had been instructed. Her stepmother and stepsisters were at once burned up in its fiery glare; only Vasilisa remained untouched. Her household gone, she set out into the world to look for work. An old woman in the city took her in and set to work spinning and weaving. With the help of her little doll she made the finest linen ever seen. When she asked her mistress to sell it as the price of her keep, the old woman was scandalized: such fabric as that must be given to the tsar.

The ruler was entranced by the linen's softness but could find no seamstress delicate enough to work it, so he took it back to the old woman to be made into shirts. Shaking her head in dejection, she confessed that there was only one girl in the entire land who could sew such exquisite cloth. So the tsar commanded that she be found and employed at once. By the time Vasilisa had finished the job it was clear that his hopes had not been raised in vain. So soft in their texture, so flowing in their lines, such shirts had never before been seen. Delighted, the tsar asked to meet their maker: he was overwhelmed by Vasilisa's beauty, and married her there and then.

107

RICHES REAL AND IMAGINED

The gold and silver citadels of Slavic folktale were the very stuff of fantasy for peasants living in the bleak Russian countryside. For the royalty who ruled over them, however, fairytale castles were a sumptuous reality. Between the sixteenth and eighteenth centuries, the architects of the Russian empire built churches and palaces fit for any magical king or queen. While styles were imported from abroad, their execution soon took on a distinctly Russian feel, with high tent roofs and onion domes dominating walls bedecked in brightly coloured *kokoshniki* tiles – and baroque and rococo forms that reached their apogee in a land whose folktales told of beneficent monarchs ruling distant realms, beyond the reach of all but the most heroic mortals.

Above: In Russia, the domes and cubes of Byzantine churches became taller and more pointed – a practical defence against the weight of northern snowfalls. Moscow's Verkhne-Spasskii Cathedral, set within the Kremlin walls, was built in 1678 and proved to be one of the last buildings designed with such typical forms, before Peter the Great began importing baroque styles from Europe.

Top: The fairytale shapes of St Basil's Cathedral, commissioned by Ivan the Terrible in 1555, stunned visitors to Moscow. Photo by Roger Fenton, *c.*1852.

Right: An elaborately tiled stove dominates a 17th-century ante-room in the Kremlin's Terem Palace. Even with European styles in vogue, the Russian character continued to impress itself on its buildings.

Left: Under the guidance of Catherine the Great, even the classicism of Scottish architect Charles Cameron became grandiose. In what was known as *Tsarskoe Selo*, or "the imperial village", the tsarina wished to escape the regal pomp of St Petersburg to enjoy a more simple rural life just outside the city. To compensate for the small, cosy rooms, however, Cameron covered walls with mirrors throughout Catherine's palace, reflecting the splendour of the monarch herself and the power at her command.

Above: Catherine also commissioned French architect Vallin de la Mothe to design the Hermitage in St Petersburg in 1764, maintaining the ornate splendour of her other buildings.

TALES OF WONDER, MAGIC AND SORCERY

Today's city-dweller is scarcely aware of the elements' hostility, for every aspect of life in the modern industrialized nations conspires to keep nature tame and at a safe distance. The Slavic peasantry of another age, however, were caught in an unceasing struggle with the bitter extremes of winter and summer, their lives locked in combat with an obstinately uncooperative earth.

And yet, if none knew better the harsh realities of rural life than the hard-working country folk, none has ever invested the natural world with more extravagant enchantment. For theirs was a world which resonated with all the potential of imagination and sorcery, a universe divided not between the rational and spiritual, but between the real powers of supernature and the marvellous fictions they fuelled.

For the Slavs, magic was twofold in its potency, functioning both as matter-of-fact truth and enjoyable fantasy. This love of stories was central to the Slavic spirit, and the more wildly improbable the tales were the better. By night they escaped into worlds of wonder: huddled around the stove through the long hours of the winter evenings, Slavic families would forsake reality for a world of myth whose skies were criss-crossed by flying carpets, whose horizons were ringed by magic mountains scaled by epic heroes who, advised by talking animals, wielded enchanted swords and saved beautiful princesses from tower-top prisons of silver and gold. But by day, these superstitious people would protect themselves with trusty spells – for the powers of the village sorcerer were assumed to be no more than the literal truth.

Magic thus surrounded these people from cradle to grave. But the Slavs of old would always see a clear difference between mythical fantasy and magical reality. Even when the two worlds appeared to share some feature, there were always clear distinctions. The witch of fairytale, for instance, was the *vedma,* who rode her poker with her cat at her side; but the *koldunya* was her real-life counterpart whose supernatural skill few would dare to question.

Left: **Pagan symbols mix with Christian motifs on the face of this c.11th-century amulet from Kiev. It was used in rituals to relieve pain in the womb and ensure health in childbirth.**

Opposite: **A popular print entitled** *Marvellous Wildmen Discovered by Alexander of Macedon* **which would have delighted people in Russia in the 1820s.**

111

Visions of Mystery

The marvels of the Slavs' mythical world ensured that nothing was ever quite as it seemed. With riddles, the imagination could transform the most banal objects into strange and fantastic phenomena. And through spells, matter could change shape and form utterly.

"On an island in the sea", said the old Russian riddle, "sits a bird who has seen it all. She has seen the tsar in Moscow, the king in Lithuania, the infant in his cradle and the old hermit in his cell." She is death, indiscriminate devourer of great and humble, pitiless taker of young and old.

That the Slavs should have referred to death so obliquely is perhaps in part a result of fear. But the popularity of riddles like these was also a mark of the Slavs' belief that, by simultaneously revealing and concealing a truth, the language of riddle represented the mysterious reality they saw all around them. "There is a strange script written on blue velvet parchment," suggested another riddle, "which no priest or prelate is learned enough to read." A description of the stars in the sky, this

Dew settles over a Russian river, veiling the landscape in mist. In a similarly enigmatic way, Slavic riddles and wonder tales delighted in rendering complex the seemingly obvious.

riddle also drives at the unfathomability of the world we see. Like many Slavic riddles, it hints at the deceptiveness of the objective world and the secrets within what appears most banal.

Examples abound of making the mundane romantic: there was the popular notion that the dawn was a beautiful maiden who had lost her keys, the dew, which were first ignored by the moon and then afterwards picked up, or dried, by the daytime sun; or the shepherd and his straggling flock who, in riddle, stood for the moon and stars. Metaphor here represents magic, and its power to work the transformation of forms. In this sense *zagadki*, or riddles, were near relations of *zagovory*, spells which, at a word, could change the sun into an oak tree, or a black cow into the night. Such shapeshifting was celebrated in a mythology rich in marvels, as the story of an innocent girl and her wicked sisters shows.

The Silver Saucer and the Crystal Apple

A peasant and his wife had three daughters: two were smart and sophisticated, but the third was a simple fool. One day the peasant went to market and promised to bring back gifts for the three of them. The older girls demanded rich and extravagant fabrics, but the fool asked for a silver saucer and an apple of crystal glass.

When their father came home with the gifts, the sisters laughed at the fool as she sat in a corner rolling the crystal apple around on its silver saucer. But as they looked mockingly on, they saw an entire universe take shape in the apple, with great cities and foam-flecked seas. The sisters at once grew jealous and when the fool refused to give up her gift, they began plotting her murder.

The following week they set out from home as if to gather strawberries. The two elder sisters led their simple sibling deep into the woods, and there, in a clearing, did her savagely to death with a spade. They buried her beneath a birch tree, and told their grieving father she had wandered off alone and been lost in the forest.

Not long after, a shepherd was searching for a lost lamb when he came across a little hummock bedecked with beautiful flowers. Behind them stood a clump of bullrushes, from one stem of which the shepherd decided to make himself a pipe. But when he had finished it, it began to sing of its own accord: in fluting tones it told him of a murder that had been committed – all for a silver saucer and an apple of enchanted glass.

The whole village was in uproar at the shepherd's news, and when the girl's father heard the tale, he understood at once. He asked the shepherd where he had cut his rush-pipe and there he found his youngest daughter's grave. The pipe played again, telling him how the murder had

been committed: it could only be undone, it said, by water from the tsar's sacred well. Sick at heart, the father saw his older girls' guilt and handed them over to the authorities for punishment while he set off to find the sacred well.

When he returned, he sprinkled the water on his daughter's grave and she came to life at once. She wept with joy to be restored to him, but shed tears of sorrow when she learned of her sisters' fate. She went to the tsar to sue for mercy and showed him her silver saucer and crystal apple: he could have it, she said, if he would only spare her sisters. Astounded alike by her surpassing beauty, her goodness and her simple wisdom, the tsar pleaded with the peasant's daughter to be his queen. And the fool and the emperor were married, and ruled both well and wisely side by side.

While the elder daughters coveted their sister's gift, they failed to realize that the marvels they saw conjured within the crystal apple matched the purity of the youngest girl's mind. Hers was an innocent vision which encompassed the whole world.

Witchcraft and Wizardry

Sorcery formed a part of the very fabric of Slavic life, and was not originally perceived as a singularly evil practice. Well into the nineteenth century, people in remote rural areas were as likely to call upon the local sorcerer for advice as they were the village priest.

Despite the general success of the Orthodox Church in supplanting paganism in the Slavic mind, many of the old traditions persisted in the remoter rural areas where the priest's authority would often coexist with the sorcerer's power.

The genuine piety of the people did not interfere with their faith in supernatural powers. Both priest and sorcerer could be consulted on all matters, be they of life, birth, marriage or death, for while the former could pray, the latter could divine. And while the belief in spirits of nature endured (see pages 58–77), so too would faith in the power of the wizard: it took a magician to give advice on how to appease angry spirits or seek for signs of ill-fortune and good luck.

A sorcerer would consult auguries to foretell the community's future and people's individual destinies – in business and in love. Since diseases were thought to have their origins in malign magic,

it seemed natural to turn to a magician for their cure. Just about every illness could be banished from the body, it was believed, if the right incantations were uttered and the correct rituals observed. The evil spirits which caused these conditions might be driven out by purifying water or fire. The healer's words might be accompanied by rituals of washing or of sprinkling; or he or she might fumigate the evil with a smoking brand.

Folk medicine had evolved elaborate procedures for protecting against disease. Wise men and women kept fevers from a house by washing its door-lintels and windowsills with water; comparable rituals around field boundaries helped keep

Despite the role of the Orthodox priest in people's everyday lives, the wizard retained a place in the hearts of many rural people until recent times, as shown by this watercolour of a sorcerer visiting a peasant wedding, by Vasili Maksimov.

the crops free from pests and disease. In fact, much of what the sorcerer did would be easily recognizable to the modern practitioner of alternative medicine. Many magicians even accompanied their spells with appeals to the Christian saints or the Virgin Mary.

Yet if the powers of sorcery were often used for the good of the community, no one had any illusions about their capacity to do harm. Although sorcerers were generally respected they were also deeply feared. Every conceivable ill could be attributed to their spells: not just death, disease and infertility but friends falling out and family discord. Even in the nineteenth century, law courts were recording cases brought against individuals who were accused of casting malign charms. Epilepsy, convulsions, even hiccups, were regarded as forms of diabolical possession spread by sorcery. In Russia in 1815 a peasant called Mikhail Chukharev was sentenced to public flogging for causing a bad bout of hiccups in his cousin. What to a later age would seem a ludicrously fanciful charge was taken entirely seriously by the authorities: indeed the accused himself admitted his offence, confessing to the court how he had removed the Cross from around his neck before uttering a spell over a little pile of salt. Scattered on the roadway where its intended victim was due to pass, the salt duly afflicted him with Chukharev's curse, and the desired complaint. One visitor to a village in Russia's Nizhnii Novgorod Province in 1848 was astonished to see a great crowd yelling and screaming in pursuit of an unfortunate piebald dog which villagers believed to be a witch in canine form who had caused an epidemic of cholera.

Elaborate decoration and cleansing of door-lintels and windowsills was believed to keep evil influences away from a household. This carved windowframe is from Suzdal in Russia.

The roots of Slavic sorcery lie in distant, pagan times, when the *kolduny* or *volkhvy* served the people as sorcerers, or priests. Condemned by the early Orthodox Church, these healers were quickly driven underground. But their influence remained powerful, and the Church launched repeated campaigns to destroy them once and for all. The tenth-century conversion of Russia was in fact anything but complete: though the aristocratic elite might have become Christians, the broad mass of the population remained wedded to the old ways. "In this year", stated the *Primary Chronicle* in its entry for 1024, "magicians appeared in Suzdal, and killed old people by satanic inspiration and Devil worship, saying they would spoil the harvest. There was great confusion and famine throughout all that country." Ecclesiastical courts were used to spearhead an all-out attack on what was still perceived as an influential rival religion; they were backed by kings and princes, who feared the *volkhvy* as a focus of wider political unrest. At village level, priests urged their parishioners to denounce their witches and sorcerers at confession, though for the most part with little success. Christianity may have been the official religion, but it was the *volkhvy* who remained the priests of people throughout the countryside.

The Church, however, slowly eroded the *volkhvy*'s influence by altering the way they were seen. Over time, the people's champions came to be viewed as perpetrators of evil: although they still turned to them for healings and fortune-tellings, people began laying all manner of evil circumstance at the *volkhvy*'s door. Crop failures, floods, droughts and other disasters were now

The Art of Spoiling

The Slavs believed that spells and potions held great power over our world. Around every ill, suspicions would abound as to whether the sickness was the work of a sorcerer – or even of some soul who had happened upon a magic recipe.

Where wizards and witches were active, the dangers to innocent people were all-pervasive: there was no way of knowing from where an evil attack might come.

Every animal and bird might be a sorcerer in disguise: if a pregnant woman went into the yard when there was a magpie there, it was thought her unborn child might be blighted in the womb. Food, drink and clothing might all be used as vehicles of the sorcerer's "spoiling", the unsuspected means by which the magic was transmitted.

Sorcerers cooked up their evil magic by making powders and potions from herbs and roots – the merest sprinkling in the victim's meal and his spoiling was assured. Fearsome spells could be conjured up by the magician's rites and incantations, but the most damaging spoilings might be far more prosaic affairs. A really powerful sorcerer could spoil his victim without any such ceremonial, spreading his baneful curse by a kiss, a touch or even just a malevolent glance. Stray hairs spread with clay or the mud from around a footprint were other means by which the sorcerer could gain power over his victim: hung in a little bag near the fire, the earth dried out, grew brittle and crumbled – and as it did so, the victim's life fell apart.

A lithograph of a pagan priest, after a 19th-century painting by E. Karnejeff. In his hands he holds the tools of his sorcery, a graven image and piece of cloth he will cast into the fire.

liable to be blamed on the sorcerers whose prophecies and cures had once been so sought-after. Mob witch-hunts became routine in the wake of such calamities, such a threat to public order, in fact, that the *volkhvy*'s enemies in the Church hierarchy felt obliged to call for restraint. Writing in a time of famine in the thirteenth century, Bishop Serapion of Vladimir remonstrated with his flock, first for being so simple as to believe in their sorcerers' power to bring rain, sunshine and fertility to their land and then for murdering these same magicians when the crops periodically failed.

The Dark Ways of Witchcraft

The running battle between priests and sorcerers continued into the seventeenth century: indeed it would take the brutalities of war and revolution in the twentieth century to extirpate the old folk ways entirely. As the modern era began, meanwhile, the Church found itself conflating the evil of the old ways with the shock of the new, denouncing the Renaissance in similar terms to those it had become accustomed to using against witchcraft. Slavic scholars and doctors who dabbled in the new learning were accused by conservative clerics of making pacts with the Devil. Protestantism, seen as one of western Europe's most pernicious influences, was for a long time successfully excluded from the tsar's realms: and like the Lutheran rebels, a dread sorcerer who cast spells from beyond the grave was referred to as a heretic.

Viewing the pagan ways as a threat to the very fabric of society, the aristocracy may not have honoured the old practices but they certainly feared them. Throughout the sixteenth century, Russian rulers would keep their children hidden from public view, lest some ill-wisher might injure them through a magic spell or a malevolent glance. In 1547, a terrible fire swept through Moscow which the populace blamed on witchcraft aimed against Tsar Ivan the Terrible. Princess Anna Glinskaia, it was said, had soaked human hearts in water which she then sprinkled over buildings

before setting fire to them. A male relation of hers was pursued into a cathedral by an angry mob, who killed him in his supposed sanctuary before dragging his body through the streets for all to see. Tsar Ivan himself had another opponent tortured by slow burning to make him confess his dealings with the forces of darkness.

A century later, little had changed. In 1632, Michael Romanov issued an edict preventing the import of what he believed to be accursed grain from Lithuania and, later that century, the unaccountable death of Tsar Aleksei's intended wife was put down to poisoning by witches; in the ensuing witch-hunt many innocent men and women were burned at the stake.

So prevalent was the belief in sorcery that even members of the clergy were not above availing themselves of its services. While magicians' practices could never be officially condoned, it was still possible to regard much of what they did as harmless, or even beneficial: everything from healing illness and soothsaying to finding lost or stolen goods. Into comparatively recent times the folk memory of the benign *volkhvy* had not entirely been forgotten. This meant that, though outwardly disapproving, the underlying attitude was more ambivalent than it was in a western Europe which burned "witches" in their thousands.

Such a pervasive belief in sorcery meant that a rich folklore grew up around witchcraft. It was believed that witches and wizards could control the elements. Give them half a chance and they would steal the dew and the rain. Having hoarded their spoils of moisture through weeks and months of the most agonizing drought, they were then all too likely to unleash them all in an instant, with a single destructive outburst of torrential rain.

In parts of Russia, indeed, witches were thought to steal not only the weather but the moon and stars as well, lest their pure light might otherwise mar the evil enjoyment of the witches' sabbaths that were held on remote hilltops at the time of the winter and summer solstices. Accordingly the *vedma,* or witch of song and story, was a bestial character who sported a tail and rode screaming through the air on a broom or poker.

117

Unmasking a Witch

Unlike their fictional counterparts, real witches and sorcerers could not easily be identified on sight. There were, however, ways of making them reveal themselves.

In Russia's Penza Province it was thought that a Palm Sunday candle could be used to identify a sorcerer: when lit it would cause all nearby witches and wizards to turn upside-down. Light a fire of aspen wood on Holy Thursday, went another common tradition, and sorcerers would come and beg for the ashes. Objects fresh and new helped highlight the sorcerer's presence – hence the importance of Easter as a time for unmasking them. Dressing in new clothing or holding the first egg of a young hen in the outstretched palm of a hand in church would force a sorcerer to turn and flee. In Orel Province it was believed that a set of new wheels mounted on sticks and then rolled round the yard would immediately shatter if there were a sorcerer nearby. The resulting splinters, burned at a crossroads, would cause the witch or wizard to cry out in pain.

The sorceress, shown in this 19th-century watercolour, by E. Karnejeff, was generally respected in Slavic society while the witch was reviled as insidious and secretive, the worker of black magic.

The *koldun*, however, was a real person. Such sorcerers did not conform to any stereotype: they might as easily be male as female and were as likely to be young as old. Eyewitness accounts of tailed witches do exist but such testimony seems suspect, to say the very least. Outward appearance was really no guide, as even popular folklore agreed. One man in Russia's Tula Province who faced ruin because his whole herd of cows had run completely dry stood watch one night in a despairing vigil, hoping to discover what was wrong. In the dead of night he saw a cat slink by and turn before his astonished eyes into a woman. She looked ghostly in the darkness, wearing only a white shift. She started milking the nearest cow into a leather bag she had brought with her. The peasant strode swiftly forward, swung his axe and severed her arm at the wrist. The witch at once fled whimpering into the night, and the man, well pleased with his work, went back into his house to sleep: and there he found his mother, moaning in her slumbers, blood oozing from the stump of her arm.

Witches and wizards had a passion for milk and regularly stole it from neighbours' cows: if a direct approach appeared too dangerous, they could tap into a likely victim indirectly, from some way off. By sticking a knife into a post or tree they could drain a cow at considerable distance – for the milk would run down the edge of the blade until the udder was completely empty.

Not content with drinking cows dry, they liked to spread diseases among the herds: there was a mythical figure who was known as Cow Death, portrayed as a hideous witch. Stalking the countryside each February, a withered and cadaverous old crone, she could assume other forms as required, like a black dog or a mottled calf. As a result, such animals were often killed and buried in an attempt to keep away the plague. Nor were such sacrifices confined to animals. An epidemic of cow death could come close to killing a community, wiping out in a matter of days the economic capital which had been painstakingly built up over many years.

Woe betide the man or woman over whom the merest hint of a suspicion of witchcraft hung. Hoping to ward off the worst ravages of plague, desperate villagers had been known to bury volunteer victims alive because of their reluctance to sacrifice the sorcerer they believed was to blame for all their troubles. Less extreme measures against witchcraft included, of course, the Cross of Christ, but also onions, garlic, amber and incense, none of which sorcerers were believed to like. A dead witch or wizard could be definitively dispatched with a stake of aspen – the tree on which Judas Iscariot was believed to have hanged himself. If not thus pinned down they might well continue their mischief from deep within the grave. But in the absence of any sure protection, perhaps the safest strategy was to curry favour, attempting to win the witch or wizard's goodwill through gifts and flattery – if their malice could not be prevented, at least that way it might be appeased. Hence the strange ambivalence with which the Slavic sorcerer was treated: at once an authority and an outcast; by turns respected and reviled.

Witchcraft and Wonder Tales

While witches and wizards were revered or reviled for their deeds in society at large, their presence in the fictional world of fairytale is much more assured. The figures who in real life came to represent dark dabblers in the forces of evil retained, in many tales, a more dignified stature.

In some tales, for instance, witches symbolize the darkness of night in its opposition to the day. The story of the handsome prince whose witch sister devours every person, animal and thing that comes within her reach can clearly be interpreted this way. The prince was taken safely from his

Astrological charts, like this 18th-century example from the Kolomensky Palace in Russia, celebrated the harmonious balance of the planets. Some myths, however, describe the sun and moon chasing each other hungrily across the heavens.

home before his insatiable sister had been born to be brought up in the house of the sun's sister. On reaching manhood he returned home to pay his younger sister a visit, not guessing as he awaited his dinner that she was sharpening her teeth with a view to dining upon him. A friendly mouse warned him of the danger, though, and he fled back whence he had come, his witch-sister pursuing him all the way. At last he agreed a deal with her whereby their weights would be compared, the heavier being at liberty to eat the lighter.

The witch won the contest, yet her victory was her undoing, for as she crashed onto her side of the scale, her brother shot up into the air, to land safely in the tower of the sun's sister. Left fuming on the ground, the witch could only grind her teeth and glower, cheated of her prey. In her darkness and hunger she represented the night, would-be devourer of the day, which had been saved by the intervention of the breaking dawn, the sun's protective sister.

119

The Faces of the Changeling

Slavs were in awe of sorcerers because of the power they wielded over the forces of nature. Not only could they control the weather; it was believed that they could also transform physical matter, and even manipulate their own shapes to suit their mysterious ends.

The changeling sorcerer, or *oboroten*, could take on almost any form beit a stone, a haystack or a ball of string – or even an animal or bird. Cats and dogs were common forms for the witch or wizard who wished to pass undetected; the owl was very much the Devil's bird, but the magpie was the most popular of all. This bird was banished from the city of Moscow, it is said, by the venerable Metropolitan Bishop Alexis, so often did the witches of that city adopt the form of the magpie. In the nineteenth-century, peasants strung up dead magpies on gibbets to warn away witches from their cowsheds and stables. Yet not every form was available: some were considered sacrosanct. No witch or wizard would ever be able to take on the shape of the sacred dove.

The word *oboroten* was also used to describe those whose appearance was changed against their will, those whom some sorcerer had condemned to inhabit an alien form.

These were no malevolent beasts, but tragic victims of evil magic: and the most notorious of these changelings was the *volkodlak* or werewolf.

The willing werewolf was a terrible manbeast, ravening destroyer of anything in its path. Those changed by another's curse, however, were submissive creatures, clinging hard to their old human nature, haunting their old abodes. Gentle in their ways, and protective of family and friends, they killed only when driven to desperation by hunger, and then only took livestock from distant parishes, never from their own. They dogged the steps of their old neighbours, howling and weeping in desolation, pleading for a little sympathy and for deliverance from their plight.

Some scholars have suggested that the tradition of the werewolf is descended from the ancient use of a wolf as a tribal totem. According to this theory, warriors would have worn the wolf's pelt at sacred festivals, hoping to assume the animal's warlike spirit and strength. Men would thus "become" wolves for short periods – a short symbolic step from werewolfism – and so, it is argued, this strange tradition may have begun.

Shapeshifting seems to have been central to Slavic myth. The hero Volga could change form at will, from a hawk or wolf to a great white bull or a tiny ant. A clue to his abilities lies in his name – surely a corruption of *volkh*, the old name for a benign sorcerer. Yet he was by no means the only epic hero with these powers: Slavic mythology revels in such transformations.

The art of falconry, represented on this 8th-century strap-end from Slovakia, was a revered form of mastery of beast by man. The sorcerer's control over physical form itself was seen as the greatest power of all.

One tale, for instance, tells how a poor man's son was apprenticed to a sorcerer – the only man prepared to take the boy on without a payment his father could not afford. But even the sorcerer attached a condition to his contract: if at the end of three years the father could not recognize his son, the boy would have to stay with his master for good. The father thought about this strange pledge but, deciding that it was a laughable proposition, he refused to take it seriously and agreed.

One day, however, when the apprenticeship was near its end, a little bird alighted on the ground outside the poor man's house. It promptly turned into his son, who warned his astonished father not to be so complacent about the agreement he had made. He was not his master's only apprentice, he said – there were eleven others who had been forced to stay with him forever, for their master had disguised them well. The boy then told his father that he would give him subtle signs which, if spotted, would enable him to rescue his son.

So the next day, when the father went to see the sorcerer, he was undaunted when confronted with a dozen little birds, all absolutely identical in appearance. His own son, as promised, fluttered a few inches higher than the rest: and his father picked him out easily, to the sorcerer's obvious annoyance. Next the magician showed him twelve colts, alike in every conceivable feature – but only one stamped its right forefoot, and by that sign the peasant knew his only child. When he had picked out his son from a parade of identical youths by the little fly sitting on his right cheek, the sorcerer knew he had been undone, and gave up the boy.

As they journeyed home the son decided to avail himself of the powers he had learned from his former master: seeing a wealthy nobleman driving by, he promptly took on the form of a fine

This 19th-century Polish ram mask would have been used to symbolize bestial transformation in rituals with ancient origins.

dog. His father should sell him for a good price, he said, but should under no circumstances give up his collar: if he did, said his son, he would have no means of returning home. The old man did as his son said and made the sale, but the noble was appalled when he saw him start to remove the collar from the dog. Who ever sold a dog without its collar? he asked, and, feeling that this was indeed rather mean-spirited, the peasant replaced the collar, and the nobleman rode off happily with his dog – and the peasant's son. But, fortunately, a little way down the road, the noble decided to set his dog after a hare; the son ran off to rejoin his father, and restored himself to his human form. He upbraided his father bitterly: had he not warned him not to sell the collar? If it had not been for the appearance of the hare, he said, he would have been lost to his father for good.

Before long, the youth decided that his father should sell him once again. This time he took on the form of a beautiful bird, locked up in a little cage. Again he warned his father that what they were doing was potentially dangerous: he should sell him for whatever price he could get but should under no circumstances hand over his cage. His father took him to market, where bidding for the pet was brisk. Among the crowd was the youth's old master, who recognized the peasant and

121

guessed the nature of the bird. So when he bought it, he insisted on taking the cage as well. But this time the father heeded his son's warning. The magician wrapped his purchase in a handkerchief, but by the time he reached home it had flown. Next time, he knew, he would have to do rather better to secure his former charge.

The opportunity came the following week, when the old man appeared in the market with a fine horse for sale. Despite keen competition, the sorcerer bid highest and bought it, but protested volubly when the old man attempted to remove its bridle. Sell the horse and you sell its bridle, all the other horse dealers agreed, and the old man had no alternative but to hand it over with the horse.

Back in his old master's power, the boy-horse was tied up tightly in the sorcerer's yard, but by good fortune the magician's daughter took pity on him. Seeing how closely he had been tethered, she loosened his reins a little – just enough for him to slip his harness and flee homewards. Told by his weeping daughter what she had done, the sorcerer changed shape himself: a grey wolf, he ran off in pursuit of his apprentice. The horse soon came to a steep riverbank as the wolf was beginning to close on him; thinking quickly, he turned into a perch, and swam off into the current. The wolf was brought up short for a moment, but did not hesitate for long: assuming the shape of a pike, he plunged straight in and resumed his pursuit through the rushing water. The perch

This horse figure, which marked a 16th-century grave near the Croatian border with Hungary, symbolizes the proud spirit of war.

swam on and on, the pike gaining on him all the time, until he saw some maidens washing linen by a jetty. Turning into a golden ring, he rolled to the feet of one of them, a merchant's daughter: she picked it up and hid it among her clothes. But the magician was not deceived and, taking on a man's shape, he angrily demanded the ring, which he told the merchant's daughter was his own property. She hurled it down in vexation and it broke up into tiny grains of corn, whereupon the sorcerer took the form a cock and began pecking. As he did so, one grain turned abruptly into a hawk: it flung itself at the cock and tore it to pieces. With the magician finally dead, the youth was freed. His apprenticeship had taught not only him but also his father rather more than they had bargained for!

Sister Alionushka

Characters in wonder tales are as likely to become victims of the sorcerer's art through their own insatiable curiosity as they are from being the objects of a witch's spite. In one story, young Prince Ivanushka was turned into a goat after drinking from a forbidden well.

Ivanushka's loving sister, Princess Alionushka, kept him with her as her constant companion from that day forth – even when, as a beautiful young woman, she had married a great king and become his queen. But one day a wicked witch put a blight on

The Reluctant Werewolves

Werewolf stories were often more tragic than terrifying for there were few willing changelings in Slavic folklore. Most tales tell of a slighted sorcerer exacting revenge.

A Polish young man was once beloved of a witch but he scorned her passion, little guessing the danger he was in. One day, grazing his cattle in the woods, he decided he would cut some wood. As he raised his axe, however, he saw his hands becoming paws before his very eyes. He looked on helplessly while his fingernails turned into curling claws, and great tufts of hair started to sprout all over his body. When he ran to his cows, intending to herd them quickly home, they stampeded in abject terror. He sought to call them back, but could only howl. To his horror, he realized he was now a wild and lonely werewolf.

In Belorussia, it was said, a slighted sorcerer once blighted a whole wedding feast, not allowing anybody to leave in the form in which they had arrived. The groom and other men were changed into werewolves, the women into chattering magpies. The bride herself was left until last: then she became a cuckoo, and searched for her husband far and wide, seeking him endlessly with the same monotonous, melancholy cry.

ust as the farmer began to cut wood in the forest, he ₑlt hairs sprout from his hands and face. And when his ₐttle fled in terror he knew his change was complete.

the king and his family. The royal gardens withered and died; even the queen herself was taken ill with a debilitating disease. Finally the sorceress abducted Alionushka, tied a stone round her neck and tossed her into the sea, then set herself up in the royal palace in the queen's place.

The king failed to spot the imposter, so glad was he to see his wife's health apparently restored. But when she had the goat banished from her company he was amazed at this change in attitude. He went along with his beloved's wishes, however, and even agreed when she demanded that the animal be slaughtered. At the last moment, though, he took pity, and allowed the goat to go down to the shore for a final drink of water.

Twice the goat went to the water's edge and called to his sister for help – but on each occasion he found he was calling out in vain. When at last an answer came, she told him she was trapped where she was, weighed down by the sorceress's stone. A third time he went down to stand among the breakers, and the king, whose curiosity had been awakened by the goat's strange behaviour, followed to see what he was doing. This time Alionushka came swimming to the surface, to be reunited with her brother and husband at last. As the royal gardens burst once more into life, the royal couple returned joyfully home with the goat. And the sorceress was burned at the stake, never more to bring unhappiness into the kingdom.

123

A Fierce Menagerie

Of all the fabulous creatures which populate Slavic mythology, none could be more sinister than the writhing, twisting snake or its hideous relation – the multi-headed dragon. But these were just a few of the beasts encountered by mythic heroes.

All evil might be represented by the fantastic figure of the serpent or dragon: in its writhing coils it appeared to encompass everything that was dark and vile. The tale of "Dobrynya and the Dragon" (see page 130), an allegorical epic of Russia's Christian salvation, saw this monster as symbolizing a hideously benighted pagan past. Yet it was a more appropriate, and more ambivalent, symbol than Slavic Christians may ever have realized. For in the earliest times the snake possessed wider, more positive associations.

Whatever their significance in the mythological literature, snakes were prized as good-luck omens in the Slavic home. Well into the nineteenth century Russian peasants kept them as pets, while in Polish households people regarded them like protective *domovye*, seeking to maintain their favour with offerings of food and drink. This friendly regard would appear to belie any claim that the snake was intrinsically loathsome, even within a Slavic culture whose mythology did indeed demonize it as the Devil's creature.

However conditioned we ourselves may have become by the attitudes of the Christian West, many other civilizations have seen serpents in an altogether kinder light. There is evidence to suggest that it was formerly so among the Slavs, for some scholars have claimed that the serpent was once closely associated with the thunder god. The deity responsible for creating mountains and for

The dragon was the mythically imagined form of the snake, which was once a benign force allied to ancient deities. These pagan echoes, however, made multi-headed dragons, like the one above, c.1906, singularly evil.

hurling down bolts of lightning also launched storms of life-giving rain onto the earth beneath him. Awesome as his strength was, pagan belief did not characterize it as being wielded destructively: only with the coming of Christianity did his powers become identified with those of evil.

That identification was made, however, and grew stronger as each century passed. The winged snake which carried clouds across the sky may once have been seen as bringing life-sustaining rain; now, however, the emphasis was on the role it played in blotting out the sun's light and warmth. The beautiful virgins who in countless tales were kept prisoner in enchanted castles by terrible dragons represented in their fresh femininity the fertile potential of the earth. A symbol, therefore, of winter and the annual death of nature, the snake's associations in such stories were strongly negative. Only its slaying by the heroic prince could deliver the captive princess and unlock the life and hope of spring. By the same token, the serpent could stand for the sun's daily death each nightfall. According to one *skazka,* the twelve-headed dragon slain by the hero Ivan Popyalof and his brothers had stolen the daytime, condemning the whole kingdom to perpetual darkness. When the final neck was severed and the monster fell twitching to the floor, the whole realm was flooded by cleansing light.

In tales of the triumph of life over death, the serpent always ended up playing the villain's part. One of the most peculiar of such tales, from Russia, tells of the brothers and sisters of Pokatigoroshek. The story starts with a girl's abduction as she took food to her brothers who were working in the forest. A seven-headed serpent carried her off and kept her prisoner in his home. Her elder brother set off to bring her back and when he arrived at the dragon's lair, he was made welcome by her abductor. But soon afterwards, the serpent's mood hardened. When his young guest proved unable to eat the bread and beans of iron which he was offered as a meal, the dragon felt slighted; and when the man refused to oblige his host by chopping up a huge log with his bare hands and burning it without fire, the

intemperate snake lost its patience and, in a sudden fit of anger, killed him on the spot. It then dropped its victim's eyes into a bubbling cauldron and hung his body from a wooden beam.

Not long afterwards, the younger brother set off in search of his two siblings: he, however, was no more fortunate, and met the same terrible fate. As their mother wept at home, bemoaning the loss of her beloved children, a pea came rolling into the room where she sat, crossed the floor and stopped at her feet. Recognizing that this was a gift from God, she ate it and, in time, bore a son, whom she named Pokatigoroshek, "rolling pea".

The son grew up into a fine young man and as soon as he could, he set off in search of his brothers and sister. Before long he came to the serpent's cottage and made short work of the iron food he was offered by the dragon. But once he had chopped up and burned the great log, his hidcous host attacked him. The whole forest seemed to shake as the young man and the serpent wrestled to the death. Pokatigoroshek finally prevailed, squeezing the life out of the writhing snake. Freeing his sister from her confinement, he drew the Water of Life from the well to revive his dead brothers and they all went home in triumph.

The image of the snake works its way through nearly all aspects of Slavic folklore, in both stories and artwork. This decorative serpent is taken from Vasnetsov's 1899 illustrations to Pushkin's tale "Oleg and the Magician".

Bears, Birds and other Beasts

Snakes were by no means the only animal forms to stalk Slavic myth: bears, wolves, frogs, birds and a host of other magical creatures also wander these colourful imaginative landscapes. Although these animals abound in the Slavic myths, their precise significance is not always easy to explain.

Some believe the association of the bear, or *medvyed,* with the old thunder god to have been based on its passion for honey, or *med,* since that was the food of the ancient Aryan gods. That the mighty bull should also be identified with the rumbling thunder is readily enough understood, as is the association of the hawk and the eagle, who traversed the high clouds in their soaring flight.

Pigeons too were seen to ride effortlessly on the storm: they too were from antiquity associated with the thunder god, though Christians identified them also with the dove of the Holy Ghost. Killing a pigeon was considered a great crime in many areas, one which was liable to be punished by cattle plague or fire. So sacred was the swan that its shooting was a strong taboo: a child who so much as saw a swan which had been killed was doomed to die. Although protected by tradition, the swan's beauteous form could still conceal great evil: one old Bulgarian tale told of a youth attacked by a *vila* or *rusalka* who had assumed the shape of an elegant swan. The brave young man wrestled her to the ground and carried her home to be his wife, tearing off her beating right wing and locking it safely away. They lived happily together until, at the christening of their son, she was called upon to dance and claimed that she could not do so without her missing wing. The wing was duly restored to her, but she promptly flew away to freedom, heedless alike of her husband's tears of grief and the cries of her hungry child.

Tsar Medvyed, King of the Bears

Four animals associated with thunder practise against one another in the strange story of Tsar Medvyed, the cantankerous King of the Bears.

Tsar Medvyed was a mighty ruler who governed his dominions with all the force in his power.

He once exacted a cruel tribute from a human king, by requiring his son and daughter to live with him as his servants, pandering to his every whim.

The king, however, rebelled at this treatment, and attempted to conceal his beloved children to keep them safe. But the bear king found them cowering in their underground hiding-place and carried them roughly away.

The next day, however, a hawk went out hunting and saw the children unguarded in Tsar Medvyed's lair. The bird swooped down and, taking the prince on his right wing and the princess on his left, flew off to return them to their father.

But the bear looked up and saw the hawk escaping with his precious prisoners: he thundered angrily and dashed his head violently against the ground. The earth shook for miles around and a jagged lightning-bolt shot high into the air: it singed the hawk's wings, and he was forced to drop his human cargo.

The following morning, the bear went out again, and this time an eagle saw him go. He swooped down, set the prince and princess free and was bearing them through the air to safety when he too was brought down by a bolt of lightning hurled by the angry tsar.

On the third day, however, a bull-calf found the children unattended. He took them on

The Firebird and Princess Vasilisa

The mysterious and elusive Firebird figures in several Slavic tales. One Russian story tells of a young huntsman, too eager to please the king his master, who found the Firebird's beautiful golden feather when riding through the forest one day. His horse warned him to leave the plume where he saw it – it would bring him nothing but trouble – but the young man could not resist picking it up and presenting it to his lord. The king was delighted with his gift, but immediately started coveting the bird from which it came. He gave the huntsman a cruel ultimatum: he must catch the Firebird and bring it to him, or else pay for his failure with his head.

The young man was filled with consternation and began to fear for his life, but his faithful horse reassured him: he told him to strew a great field with corn and then wait patiently for the hungry Firebird to arrive and eat its fill.

Sure enough, the bird quickly came. As soon as it landed, the resourceful horse rushed out and pinned its wing down with his hoof. The hunter picked the bird up and took it off to the king. He was so impressed that he promptly demanded that the young man go out and fetch him a bride. Princess Vasilisa he wanted, a woman of enchanting beauty who lived at the very end of the Earth. The hunter would be well rewarded if he brought her back; if he failed he would pay with his life.

Again the huntsman wept with fear and once more his horse told him not to worry but to set out a rich banquet on a seaside clifftop. Passing by in her silver boat, Princess Vasilisa saw the enticing spread: she could not resist putting in to shore and tasting the fare. One glass of enchanted wine and the princess slept; the huntsman called to his grazing horse, and they set off back to the palace with the prize the king had sent them for.

his back and galloped off through the forest. Tsar Medvyed heard them go, and stormed and shouted in rage. But the bull-calf ignored him and kept running on with the young prince and princess on his back. The bear king flung his lightning bolts but they bounced harmlessly off the bull-calf's hide; he set the earth trembling but the beast charged on undaunted and carried them to safety.

The bear guarded his royal servants jealously but was confounded by his fellow forest beasts. The hawk, who first rescued the children, was felled by Medvyed's bolts of lightning, before the bull-calf finally set them free.

The king rejoiced at his good fortune, but when the princess awoke she was furious at her abduction. She would not marry the king without her own wedding gown, she said, and that lay far out in the middle of the sea beneath a great stone. The king called immediately to his huntsman, and sent him off to recover it. Once more his horse offered to help him. They went down to the shore where the horse trapped a crab beneath his hoof. The crab pleaded for mercy, promising any favour in return so the horse charged it with finding Princess Vasilisa's bridal shift. The crab called together all its relations to assist it in its search and in no time at all they had found it.

But the princess, it seemed, had one more demand to make: she now asked that the huntsman bathe in boiling water. His horse set a charm upon him, to keep him safe from harm, and he emerged from the seething cauldron a paragon of beauty. So impressed was the king that he promptly plunged in himself and was killed at once. Princess Vasilisa fell in love with the brave huntsman on the spot. They were married and ruled together in his old master's kingdom.

Prince Ivan and the Grey Wolf

In another story the Firebird made a nuisance of itself, stealing the golden apples from the garden of King Vyslav Andronovich. He set his three sons to keep watch on his trees and catch it if it came to cause trouble again. Prince Dimitri watched the first night – and promptly fell asleep; Prince Vasily watched the second night and fared no better. The third night, however, Prince Ivan watched until suddenly the whole night seemed flooded with a dazzling golden light. The Firebird alighted in the tree and started picking apples. Ivan crept quietly up and grabbed it by the tail, but it managed to slip from his grasp: he was left hold-

The Firebird is one of the most beguiling figures from the mythical menagerie. It has retained its charm in the 20th-century, inspiring paintings like this laquered piece by Belov, _c._1982, as well as Stravinski's ballet _The Firebird_.

ing a single miraculous feather. When he saw the prize the king was more eager than ever to have the bird and sent his elder sons into the world to find the fantastic creature and catch it at all costs.

Prince Ivan was eager to go too. At last his father reluctantly agreed and he rode off into the world to try his fortune. He had not ridden far when he saw a pillar with an inscription: those who went left, it said, would be killed although their horses would get through unscathed; those who went right would be spared themselves but lose their horses. The prince took the right-hand road, and before very much time had elapsed, a huge grey wolf bounded up and snatched the horse from beneath him.

The disconsolate Ivan toiled on, increasingly footsore, and in time the wolf appeared and spoke to him courteously. It apologized for eating his horse and offered to carry him on its own back: it took him straight to the stone walls of a magic garden. Inside, in a golden cage, the Firebird could be seen. It was there for the taking, the wolf assured him. He must not, however, so much as touch a bar of the cage – if he did, King Dolmat's men would assuredly capture him.

The prince did as he had been instructed, and was just leaving with his prize when he began to think how much more convenient it would be to take the Firebird in its cage. He reached out to take it and a thunderous cacophony rang out. Guards came running to catch him and carry him before the king. The ruler was furious with the prince for trying to steal what he would gladly have given him as a gift. He must now expiate his crime by going to a neighbouring kingdom whose sovereign, King Afron, had a magnificent horse with a golden mane; the prince was to bring it back to the royal palace.

The wolf ran like the wind with Prince Ivan on its back until they reached the stable in which Afron's golden-maned horse was stalled. He could simply take it, the wolf said, but must be sure to leave its bridle. Again the prince thought he knew better, and removed the bridle from the wall: it clattered and jingled, and he was soon caught and

129

Dobrynya and the Dragon

Dobrynya personified all the qualities of the Christian hero and his combat with the dragon Goryinch is often seen as a fight against pagan darkness. He was, however, a far from perfect hero.

One hot summer's day, Dobrynya, ignoring his mother's warnings, plunged into the River Puchai to bathe. But as he splashed about in the refreshing water, the heavens opened to disgorge a huge dragon with three heads and seven great claws of copper. The terrible beast, Goryinch, then spoke: it had heard much of young Dobrynya, and how he was destined to save his country by slaying it, but Goryinch would now show who the hero really was. Dobrynya felt a moment of panic, but quickly regained his accustomed poise: the dragon should win its victory, he said defiantly, before it began boasting. Grabbing the hat he had left on the shore, he weighted it with sparkling sand and used its brim as a blade to cut off one of the dragon's heads. As he made ready to cut off the other two, the beast pleaded for mercy, promising never to harm Russia or its people again.

Such was his own honesty that Dobrynya did not doubt for a single moment that Goryinch would keep its solemn word. He was astonished and enraged, therefore, when only a few days later he heard that the dragon had stolen Zabava Putatishna, the niece of Prince Vladimir of Kiev. Far more furious still, however, was Prince Vladimir himself, appalled that Dobrynya should have let the dragon off so lightly. He ordered the hero to go to the Sorochinsk Mountains where Goryinch had its lair; he must kill the dragon this time and not come back without Princess Zabava.

The warrior journeyed far into the hills until he found himself before the dragon's home. Serpents swarmed about him but Dobrynya killed them all. When Goryinch came out to meet him, man and monster fought fearlessly for three days and nights.

Finally Dobrynya prevailed, and the dragon lay dead before him. He forced his way into the monster's lair and found Princess Zabava, along with forty captive peoples who had been chained there for generations in utter darkness. They followed him forth in their thousands, blinking in the bright sunshine, their freedom finally won thanks to Russia's great hero. They all bowed down in grateful homage as Dobrynya set Zabava behind him on his horse, and the couple began their joyful journey back to Kiev.

Dobrynya frees Zabava and the forty enchained peoples, from Vodovozov's 1941 edition of "Goryinch the Dragon". The Christian overtones of this dragon-slaying story helped make Dobrynya a Russian hero as popular as St George.

Whereas dragons and snakes were used to portray the power of evil, or pagan, influences, birds were often the chosen forms for more spiritually benign symbols. This 12th-century fresco from Smolensk suggests the majestic flight of the soul to Heaven after death. The fowl hold Christian symbols in their beaks, underlining their divine associations.

carried before King Afron. He too was angry that Ivan had attempted to rob him, and he also bade the young man do a service for him to repay his wrong. He commanded Ivan to journey to the end of the Earth where the beautiful Princess Elena lived, and bring her back to be his bride.

The youth set off with the wolf, and in time they reached the garden where Elena was walking: the wolf ran into the palace grounds and spirited her away from her attendants. As they journeyed back to Afron's kingdom, however, Prince Ivan's heart grew heavy: he himself had fallen in love with the fair Elena. The wolf offered to help him yet again, taking on the princess's form itself: Ivan gave it to King Afron who was thoroughly delighted. He cheerfully gave Prince Ivan the precious horse, and he set off with the real Elena.

The grey wolf stayed with Afron for three days before escaping. It caught up with the prince and princess and they journeyed on to Dolmat's kingdom together, but by now Prince Ivan was realizing he did not want to give up the golden-maned horse. Once again the wolf helped him, taking on the horse's form itself. King Dolmat was deceived, and quite delighted. He handed over the Firebird, and Prince Ivan went on his way; a few days later the wolf-horse threw its royal rider and set off to rejoin its companions.

Arriving at the place where it had devoured Prince Ivan's horse, the wolf bade him farewell. The prince and princess rode on together and soon lay down to sleep by the roadside. Without his friend and protector, the prince was easy prey when his envious brothers came and found him where he was sleeping. Not only did he have the Firebird, but he had a wondrous horse and a beautiful woman too. They killed him on the spot and took his prizes with them.

A month later, the grey wolf came upon Ivan's body as the ravens were gathering round to eat it. It caught one young raven beneath its giant paw and made as if to tear it apart, until its father begged it to show some mercy. The wolf agreed on condition that the raven flew to the end of the world and brought back a vial of the Water of Life which was to be found there.

The raven did as it had been ordered, and the wolf sprinkled the water on the prince, who promptly got up and shook himself as if he had only been sleeping. He rode back to his father's palace on the wolf's back, and strode into the hall to claim his bride. Princess Elena vouched for his story and told the king what the older princes had done. He threw them into a deep dungeon for their crimes. But Ivan and Elena were wed that very day, and lived together happily ever after.

131

CLASSICAL FANTASIES

For centuries, opera and ballet were the preserves of the Russian aristocracy, genteel recreations whose classical tales, orchestrated by Europeans, steered well clear of the vulgarities of popular taste. In 1836, however, the Russian composer Mikhail Glinka wrote *A Life for the Tsar*, an opera which shunned Italian influences in favour of native folk melodies and Russian subject matter. Audiences were at first appalled, but Glinka's plundering of Slavic folklore caught the imagination of the middle classes and the course of Russian music was set for the rest of the century: Borodin, Mussorgsky and Rimsky-Korsakov were all to draw heavily on folk traditions. This trend spread throughout the Slavic lands: Chopin plundered Polish legends for his *Mazurkas* and *Ballades*, and the Czech composer Anton Dvorak followed his *Slavonic Dances* with *Rusalka* in 1901. In the twentieth century, the tradition was continued by Sergei Prokofiev and Igor Stravinsky, whose *Firebird* testifies to the enduring harmony between classical music and folktale.

Above left: Costume for a sea urchin from Rimsky-Korsakov's unrealized opera *Sadko*, by Leon Bakst. The story told of the Sea Tsar who delighted in Sadko's playing of the *gusli*.

Right: Bedrich Smetana was the first Czech composer to exploit folklore. In 1870 he wrote about the legendary queen of Bohemia, Libusa, drawn here by Vitezlav Masek.

Above: Stage design for Act One of Igor Stravinsky's *Petrushka*, drawn by Aleksandr Benois. The ballet tells the story of the owner of a St Petersburg puppet theatre who brings three dolls to life. The Harlequin, Petrushka, falls in love with the Ballerina who prefers the Moor. In the ensuing tale of unrequited love, the Moor slays Petrushka, leaving the puppet owner to rue his magic powers.

Right: Costume for *The Firebird*, designed by Leon Bakst, one of the most influential associates of Diaghilev's famous Ballets Russes. Stravinsky's interest in folklore led him to create this ballet in 1910. It draws on a number of fairytales involving the Firebird, and tells of Prince Ivan's repeated attempts to catch the enchanting bird before falling helplessly in love with it.

THE LEGACY OF SLAVIC MYTH

Despite centuries of Christian influence and decades of Communist rule, Slavic culture retains much that owes its origins to the world of folklore and mythology. Indigenous art forms, in design, folktale or epic poetry, have influenced a wide range of contemporary mediums – and some have spread throughout Europe and beyond.

The bug-eyed monster of capital confronts workers in a poster from 1918 entitled "Death to Worldwide Capitalism". Mythical creatures were a favourite motif for social evils and workers were often pictured battling them like the epic heroes of old.

The propaganda posters of Soviet Communism owed much to earlier art forms: if the famed pictures of Lenin recall the form of the traditional icon, then their dramatic, narrative images and populist slogans bear the influences of *lubok* painting (see pages 78–79). Fairytale fuelled the golden age of Russian opera (see pages 132–33) and folk art, revived in Russia in the 1930s, offered a source of nationalist pride for a regime which sought to champion the nobility of the common worker.

The reawakening of interest in indigenous culture was linked to the emergence of political nationalism. In late nineteenth-century Europe, this was expressed in the pan-Slav movement, an idealistic, and ultimately unworkable, attempt to unite all Slavic peoples in a single consciousness.

The idea of a unified Slav people was first suggested by the seventeenth-century Croat priest Juraj Krizanic who led a mission to Russia in 1647 with the aim of converting Orthodox Russians to Catholicism. By the 1870s, Krizanic's ideas had become fashionable with Russian intellectuals who aimed to promote a glorious Russian empire unified by Orthodox Christians under the rule of the tsar. The religious, cultural and even linguistic contradictions within such a movement soon became obvious and pan-Slavism faded away, unable to reconcile the conflicting interests of the disparate Slavic countries.

But if the political visions of the Slavs failed to make a lasting cultural impression, then their imaginative fictions most certainly did. For while the characters of Slavic folktale were gracing the stages of opera and ballet companies across the continent, darker spectres from Slavic folklore were stirring in the minds of Europeans.

Christopher Lee makes his terrifying debut in the title role of *Dracula* in 1958. Although nearly 200 films have already been made about this most famous vampire, the public's appetite for him appears far from sated.

The Rise of the Vampire

In the nineteenth century, when the intellectuals' pan-Slavic movement was at its height, the Slavic vampire was already legendary in western Europe.

Stories of attacks by bloodsucking revenants had been in popular circulation since the eleventh century – and most of them had been encouraged by the very people who sought to dismiss them as fictions. Over the centuries, stories of ghoulish visitations were studiously collected and published by scholars and clerics who were keen to demonstrate that the fearsome creature of the night was mere superstition. But reports of vampire attacks were still greeted with fervent speculation as late as 1732, when Serbian police publicized one famous outbreak of vampirism.

In the late eighteenth and early nineteenth centuries, however, the notion of the vampire, under attack from both scientists and clerics, became purely imaginative. Writers and artists of the Romantic movement, reacting against the prevailing rationalism of the age, were drawn towards the supernatural and the beliefs of past times – and the figure of the eternally damned and sorrowing soul had a natural attraction for them.

The Romantics reinvented the vampire as an image of death, particularly in the form of the *femme fatale*, a seductive young woman in whose arms unsuspecting youths would meet their end. Vampire attacks had once been understood as horrific and frenzied incidents but now the image of the night creature began to be associated with seduction – and swooning sexual encounters became a major motif in later treatments. The term *femme fatale* came in time to mean simply an attractive woman – one whose charms could tempt a man to ruin. In the early twentieth century, these temptresses even became known as "vamps". It was indeed an old Russian tradition that the shapeshifting Devil took pleasure in distracting devout peasants at Easter by appearing to them in the form of a scantily clad young woman while they trudged to church.

The vampire found its place in English literature following the celebrated night in Geneva in June 1816 when the English poet Lord Byron and his companions sat up until dawn telling each other spinechilling ghost stories. Finding they had a taste for such lurid tales, they agreed to hold a contest to see who could come up with the most terrifying narrative. With Byron were fellow poet Percy Bysshe Shelley, Shelley's wife Mary and Byron's secretary Dr John Polidori. Mary Shelley's effort for the competition was the horror story *Frankenstein*, or *The Modern Prometheus*, published two years later in 1818. Byron's attempt was a vampire story, which he left unfinished. His tale, however, later inspired Polidori to write his own, with an aristocratic vampire hero named Lord Ruthven. When Polidori's *The Vampyre: A Tale* was printed in April 1819 in the English *New Monthly*

135

The tradition of epic poetry found its 20th-century equivalent in the cinematic historical dramas of the 1930s and 1940s. Here Nikolai Cherkassov plays the scheming Tsar Ivan in Sergei Eisenstein's unfinished bio-pic, *Ivan the Terrible*, made in 1945.

Magazine, the publisher falsely claimed that its author was none other than Byron himself, a coup which brought it wide attention.

Polidori's narrative, deviously miscredited, sparked a fashion in European literary and dramatic circles for Gothic tales of horror and blood-sucking. In France *The Vampyre* was twice adapted for the stage, by Charles Nodier in 1820 and the elder Alexandre Dumas in 1852. In Britain the serial bloodthirsty adventures of *Varney the Vampyre* were a hit both in the "penny dreadful" magazines and when collected in a huge single volume, published anonymously in 1847. The craze inspired another significant work, the novella *Carmilla* published in 1871 by the Irish newspaperman Joseph Sheridan Le Fanu. It featured a *femme fatale* vampiress who chose only young female victims.

In 1897 appeared the most celebrated of all vampire stories, the one that would win the creature a cherished place in twentieth-century popular culture: *Dracula*. The novel was by Irishman Bram Stoker, who at the time was working as stage manager of the Royal Lyceum Theatre in London. When he set out to write a vampire tale, Stoker read widely in both Slavic folklore and the literature of the occult.

Stoker's book was a great success, but Count Dracula's transformation into a modern icon did not truly start until 1927. A stage version by Hamilton Deane, which had first played in a theatre in Derby in 1924, was put on in London three years later and was a hit, transferring that autumn to Broadway. Its New York star was a lugubrious-looking European by the name of Bela Lugosi – born appropriately enough in Transylvania. In 1931 Lugosi repeated the role in Hollywood for Universal Studios. The resulting film *Dracula*, directed by Tod Browning, catapulted the eery, cloaked count into public consciousness. But the Hollywood *Dracula* was not the first vampire film: that honour goes to the German director F. W. Murnau whose *Nosferatu, The Vampire* opened in 1922. It too was a version of the Dracula myth, but because Murnau did not have permission for his adaptation he was obliged to change the names of the principal characters – and the famous count became Nosferatu.

More than 160 feature films have been made of the Dracula story, many of which have starred the tall, urbane British actor Christopher Lee. He took over from Bela Lugosi as the dominant screen image of the count, beginning in 1958 with *Dracula*, and made a further ten appearances as the cloaked seducer. In 1992 another British actor, Gary Oldman, filled the role in Francis Coppola's film *Bram Stoker's Dracula*, which presented itself as a return to Stoker's original novel. But even this was not the last word – for three years later, Tom Cruise played a vampire in the successful *Interview with a Vampire,* suggesting that this particular creature from Slavic folklore will be stalking our screens for some time to come.

Heroes for the Modern Age

Within Russia itself, cinema proved the saviour of another strand of Slavic mythology: the historical epic. As Marxism insisted on down-playing the role of the individual in history, heroic characters were frowned upon by the authorities in the years immediately after the 1917 revolution. In propaganda, epic feats were accomplished by the proletariat, working in glorious, impersonal harmony.

The ancient tradition of telling heroic tales, however, was not to be submerged for long, and a once-oral art-form was soon taken up by the popular new medium of cinema. Mixing social realism with historical romanticism, Russian film-makers began producing a series of epic, and often ground-breaking, films dealing with themes worthy of any *bylina*: directors like Sergei Eisenstein (*The Battleship Potemkin* 1926, and *Alexander Nevsky* 1938), Vladimir Petrov (*Peter the Great* 1937) and Mark Donskoi (*The Gorki Trilogy* 1938–40), transformed cinema into the defining medium of Russian national culture.

With the fall of Communism, Slavic countries have been exposed once again to western influences offering younger generations more material dreams. But the tales forged by their ancestors will surely survive, as they have through the generations of Slavs who have dwelt amid the great visionary expanse of the eastern European plain.

The feats of the cosmonauts provided further epic themes for Russian art. Here Yuri Gagarin's conquest of space is celebrated in Belov's *Space Brothers*, c.1980. The figures on horseback carry the symbols of Soviet Russia triumphantly into space.

137

Glossary

bannik (sing.), banniki (pl.)
Malicious Slavic spirit of the bathhouse.

bogatyr (sing.), bogatyri (pl.)
Russian heroes from epic poetry.

boyare Officals who worked as bureaucrats for local princes in the social hierarchy of Kievan Rus.

bylichka (sing.), bylichki (pl.) Tales of the spirit world which purport to be eyewitness accounts.

bylina (sing.), byliny (pl.) Russian epics which were maintained by an oral tradition for centuries before being written down.

domikha (sing.) Wife of the *domovoi*.

domovoi (sing.), domovye (pl.) Domestic spirit of the house, sometimes referred to as "grandfather". Linked to ancestor worship.

dvoeverie Dual faith – the name given to the period after the tenth-century conversion of Kievan Rus when Christianity lived side-by-side with paganism in the hearts of Slavic peasants.

dvorovoi (sing.), dvorovye (pl.) Spirit of the farmyard.

gusli Russian stringed instrument for playing devotional music.

kokoshniki Colourful tiles used in traditional Russian architecture.

koldun (masc.), koldunya (fem.), kolduny (pl.) A traditional Russian sorceror.

leshii (sing.), leshie (pl.) Spirit of the woods who can lead travellers astray.

lubok (sing.), lubki (pl.) Woodcut prints whose popular appeal lasted until the end of the nineteenth century.

lugovik (sing.), lugoviki (pl.) Spirit who watches over the open meadows.

nechistaya sila The "unclean force" Russian peasants identified as both the evil spirits of paganism and the Devil of Christianity.

ovinnik (sing.), ovinniki (pl.) Spiteful spirit of the barn.

polevoi (sing.) Male spirit of the fields, noted for his unkempt appearance.

poludnitsa (sing.) Female spirit of the fields. She guards the noonday curfew.

rusalka (sing.), rusalki (pl.) Tragic female spirit of the water.

skazka (sing.), skazki (pl.) Traditional Russian fairytales.

smerd (sing.), smerdy (pl.) Literally "stinking ones" – the farmers who were free men in the social hierarchy of Kievan Rus.

vedma Traditional fairytale witch.

vodyanoi (sing.), vodyanye (pl.) Male spirit of the water.

volkh (sing.), volkhvy (pl.) Benign sorcerer who acted as a pagan priest.

zagadka (sing.), zagadki (pl.) Russian riddles that were used as entertainment.

zagovry Magic spells or enchantments used in the art of spoiling.

For More Information

American Association of Teachers of Slavic and East European Languages
University of Southern California
3501 Trousdale Parkway
THH 255L
Los Angeles, CA 90089-4353
(213) 740-2734
Website: www.aatseel.org
Founded in 1941, the American Association of Teachers of Slavic and East European Languages works to advance the study and promote the teaching of Slavic and East European languages, literatures, and cultures on all educational levels.

Association for Slavic, East European, and Eurasian Studies
203C Bellefield Hall
University of Pittsburgh
Pittsburgh, PA 15260-6424
(412) 648-9911
Website: www.aseees.org
The Association for Slavic, East European, and Eurasian Studies is the leading international organization dedicated to the advancement of knowledge about Central Asia, the Caucasus, Russia, and Eastern Europe in regional and global contexts.

Canadian Association of Slavists
German and Slavic Studies Department
University of Manitoba
325 Fletcher Argue Building
Winnipeg, MB
R3T 2N2
(204) 474-9735
Website: www.ualberta.ca/~csp/cas/association.html
The Canadian Association of Slavists is an interdisciplinary gathering of scholars and professionals whose interests focus on the social, economic and political life of the Slavic peoples.

Department of Slavic Languages & Literatures
12 Quincy Street, Barker Center 3rd Floor
Cambridge, MA 02138
(617) 495-4065
Website: slavic.fas.harvard.edu
The Department of Slavic Languages and Literatures studies and teaches the languages, linguistics, literature, film, art, and cultural history of the Slavic world, from the medieval period up through the present.

Websites

Because of the changing nature of Internet links, Rosen Publishing has developed an online list of websites related to the subject of this book. This site is updated regularly. Please use this link to access the list:

http://www.rosenlinks.com/COW/slav

For Further Reading

Barford, P. M. *The Early Slavs: Culture and Society in Early Medieval Eastern Europe*.
Ithaca, NY: Cornell University Press, 2001.

Bulfinch, Thomas. *Bulfinch's Mythology*. New York, NY: Thunder Bay, 2014.

Dvornik, Francis. *The Slavs in European History and Civilization*.
New Brunswick, NJ: Rutgers University Press, 1992.

Fine, John V. A. *The Early Medieval Balkans: A Critical Survey from the Sixth to the
Late Twelfth Century*. Ann Arbor, MI: University of Michigan, 1983.

Glenny, Misha. *The Balkans: Nationalism, War, and the Great Powers*, 1804-2011.
New York: Penguin, 2012.

Hamilton, Edith. *Mythology: Timeless Tales of Gods and Heroes*. New York, NY: Grand Central, 2011.

Lacey, Robert. Great Tales from English History: *The Truth about King Arthur, Lady Godiva,
Richard the Lionheart, and More*. New York, NY: Little, Brown, 2004.

Lewis, Bernard, and Bernard Lewis. *Race and Slavery in the Middle East:
An Historical Enquiry*. New York, NY: Oxford University Press, 1992.

Sears, Kathleen. *Mythology 101: From Gods and Goddesses to Monsters and Mortals,
Your Guide to Ancient Mythology*. Fort Colins, CO: Adams Media, 2014.

Vlasto, A. P. *The Entry of the Slavs into Christendom; an Introduction to the Medieval History of the Slavs*.
New York, NY: Cambridge University Press, 1970.

--

Index

Page numbers in *italic* denote captions. Where there is a textual reference to the topic on the same page as a caption, italics have not been used.

141

Picture Credits

The publisher would like to thank the following people, museums and photographic libraries for permission to reproduce their material. Every care has been taken to trace copyright holders. However, if we have omitted anyone we apologize and will, if informed, make corrections in any future edition.

Key:
t top; **c** centre; **b** bottom; **l** left; **r** right

Abbreviations:

AKG	AKG London	BAL	Bridgeman Art Library, London/New York
BM	British Museum, London	DBP	Duncan Baird Publishers
ET	ET Archive, London	FAM	Folk Art Museum, Moscow
HM	Hermitage Museum, St Petersburg	RHPL	Robert Harding Picture Library
SHM	State Historical Museum, Moscow	SCR	Society for Co-operation in Russian & Soviet Studies, London
SRM	State Russian Museum, St Petersburg	V&A	Victoria & Albert Museum, London

Cover AKG London/Erich Lessing/Schloss Ambras, Innsbruck; **Cover surround** AKG/Erich Lessing/FAM; **Title page** AKG/Erich Lessing/FAM; **Contents Page** Corbis/SRM; **6** AKG; **7** Impact Photos/Christophe Bluntzer; **8** Magnum/Erich Lessing; **10** Michael Holford; **11** ET/HM; **12l** ET/HM; **12r** ET/HM; **13l** RHPL/Tretyakov Gallery, Moscow; **13r** BAL/Nationalmuseet, Copenhagen; **14** ET/Ethno Museum, Vinnitsa, Ukraine; **15** Werner Forman Archive/Biblioteca Nacional, Madrid; **16** Ancient Art & Architecture/Ronald Sheridan; **17** ET/National Historical Cultural Museum, Backchisarai, Crimea; **19** ET/SHM; **20** DBP; **21** Ancient Art & Architecture/Ronald Sheridan; **22** AKG/Erich Lessing/Hradçany Castle, Prague; **23** History Museum, Veliko Turnovo, Bulgaria; **24** TRIP/M. Barlow; **25** John Massey Stewart; **26l** Magnum/Bruno Barbey; **26r** DBP; **27l** DBP; **27c** V&A/Daniel McGrath; **27r** Images Colour Library; **28** AKG/Erich Lessing/Koszta Jozsef-Museum, Szentes, Hungary; **29** RHPL/Adam Woolfitt; **30/31** Planet Earth Pictures/Steve Bloom; **32** Jürgens Ost & Europa-Photo; **33** Corbis/SRM; **35** Corbis/Paul Almasy; **38** ET/KMA; **39** NHPA/Pierre Petit; **40** Corbis/SRM; **41** V&A/Daniel McGrath; **42–43** V&A; **44** Corbis/SRM; **45** Panos Pictures/Marie Söderberg; **47** Michael Holford/Bobrinskoy Collection, London; **48** Impact Photos/A. Johnstone; **49** Corbis/SRM; **52** Elizabeth Warner/Mike Smith; **53** V&A/Daniel McGrath; **54** Sheila Paine; **55** BAL/Private Collection; **56l** AKG; **56r** Corbis/SRM; **57** BAL/Stapleton Collection; **58** RHPL/K Gillham; **59** AKG/Erich Lessing; **60** SCR/Novosti; **61** Magnum/Ian Berry; **62** Sheila Paine; **63** AKG/Erich Lessing/FAM; **65** SHM/Elizabeth Warner; **66** AKG/FAM/Erich Lessing; **67** BAL/HM; **68** Magnum/Ian Berry; **69** Jean Loup Charmet/© Frank C Pape; **71** Corbis/SRM; **72** Tony Stone Images/Jeremy Walker; **75** ET/KMA; **76** Monastery Church of the Dormition of the Virgin, Arbanassi, Bulgaria; **77** Elizabeth Warner/Mike Smith/Saltykov-Shchedrin Public Library; **78l** BAL/Pushkin Museum, Moscow; **78–79** Michael Holford; **79t** Elizabeth Warner/Mike Smith; **79cr** BAL/Pushkin Museum, Moscow; **79br** Corbis/SRM; **80** DBP; **81** RHPL/James Strachan; **82** AKG; **83** AKG/Erich Lessing/FAM; **84** Images Colour Library; **85** Horniman Museum, London; **87** RHPL/JNW Shakespear; **88** Tony Stone Images/John Lund; **89** Horniman Museum, London; **90** Corbis/Massimo Listri/SHM; **92** Magnum/Steve McCurry; **93** BM Prints & Drawings; **95** Michael Holford/V&A; **97** AKG/Erich Lessing/Schloss Ambras, Innsbruck; **98** Mary Evans Picture Library; **101** DBP; **102** DBP; **104** Panos Pictures/David Constantine; **105** Corbis/State Russian Museum; **106** DBP; **108tr** Royal Photographic Society/Roger Fenton; **108cl** AKG/Vsevolod M. Arsenyev; **108–109b** AKG; **109t** RHPL/K Gillham; **109r** RHPL/K Gillham; **110** BM Prints & Drawings; **111** SRM; **112** Tony Stone Images/Derke/O'Hara; **114** BAL/Tretyakov Gallery, Moscow; **115** Corbis/Dean Conger; **116** BAL/Stapleton Collection; **118** BAL/Stapeleton Collection; **119** BAL/Pushkin Museum, Moscow; **120** Ancient Art & Architecture; **121** Horniman Museum, London; **122** RHPL/Michael Short; **124** Elizabeth Warner/Mike Smith; **125** DBP; **128** SCR/Novosti; **130** Elizabeth Warner/Mike Smith; **131** BAL/HM; **132tl** John Massey Stewart; **132c** BAL/Private Collection/© ADAGP, Paris and DACS, London 1999; **132br** Edimedia/Metropolitan Museum of Art, New York; **133** AKG/Erich Lessing/Musée d'Orsay, Paris; **134** ET/Institute of Slavonic Studies, London; **135** Ronald Grant Archive/Hammer Films; **136** Ronald Grant Archive/Mosfilm; **137** SCR/Novosti

1/23/17